Contents

Nationalism

I

The Anatomy of Nationalism

... Macdonagh and MacBride
And Connolly and Pearse
Now and in time to be
Whenever green is worn,
All changed, changed utterly:
A terrible beauty is born.

Yeats, 1916

The Legend and the Word

Nationalism, as the story is generally told, begins as Sleeping Beauty and ends as Frankenstein's monster. The nation—and our model here is Germany—was awakened to her destiny, not by one handsome prince, but by a variety of distinguished servitors. Romantic poets like Heine made the pulse race. Philosophers like Herder or Fichte explained who the maiden was and why she had been so long asleep. Philologists like the brothers Grimm explored the purity of her languages and bathed in the unselfconscious wisdom of her folktales. Preachers like Schleiermacher gave her a divine blessing. As for the politicians, like Bismarck and Cavour, they were as usual found to be doing the right thing for the wrong reason. And why had Sleeping Beauty been sleeping? She had been put to sleep, these servitors explained, by wicked kings and self-seeking aristocrats. If, however, we remembered back to the barbarian tribes of Roman times, the true Germany was recognisable in Tacitus' description of her lusty infant virtues. Would Sleeping Beauty live happily ever afterwards? Yes, indeed, but only after these wicked influences had been destroyed in the struggle now approaching. Yet in the course of that struggle, Sleeping Beauty began to develop some unlovely characteristics. On closer inspection, it transpired that she was in fact partly composed of lumps of flesh torn from other bodies politic. And further, the world was filling up with such creatures, all noisily awake, and all demanding attention and sympathy. Hordes of such fierce maidens filled the world, quarrelling over the lands they wished to absorb.

Does it seem frivolous to compare the foremost ideology of the modern world to a fairy tale? Nationalism invites such a comparison. It is nationalists who have appropriated fairy tales from the nursery and brought them into politics. Further, each nation needs a legend, and these legends all have a fairy-tale character about them. Above all, perhaps, nationalism is an ideology for the young. Like its cultural twin, romanticism, it is a pure-minded rejection of the compromises of adult authority. From Young Italy (whose hero was to be Garibaldi, not Cavour) in the nineteenth century to the Young Turks of the twentieth, nationalism has always found its loyal supporters among the young. Indeed, in many countries, it has created the political concept of 'youth'; where traditional modes of behaviour are still strong, young people keep respectfully silent and leave politics to the wisdom of their fathers. Politics is generally an affair of states—slow, devious and mixed in motive. Only a politics of the young could have disrupted this senile minuet, and directed political aspirations away from a hag like the state towards a beauty like the nation.

First we must inspect the word. 'Nation' has had a variety of adventures before arriving at its present eminence. It is perhaps the most successful member of a family of words which all refer to a collection of human beings and are to this limited extent synonymous. Other such words are: race, class, people, community, tribe, state, clan and society. They have all at times been more or less equally available to describe something similar, though each has at all times had additional connotations and associations which limited this availability.

Many of these words evolved their social meaning from something more abstract. 'Tribe', for example, is something composed of three parts, and referred once to the three clans of ancient Rome. It came also to be used for the twelve tribes of Israel. Such usages have grandeur, but in English 'tribe' also came to have a contemptuous undertone. Burke speaks of a 'tribe of vulgar politicians'. Here the word retains its generality (any set of persons) but suffers limitation from the contemptuous attitude of the user. In the nineteenth century, 'tribe' was appropriated as a technical term in anthropology, but it retained a pejorative political use when it supplied the stem for 'tribalism', which is sometimes used to describe a highly cohesive and suffocating political system.

'Race' has been even more closely associated with 'nation'. It began its career as a description of any group of people who claimed some kind of common descent. It was therefore appropriate in medieval times to any selfconscious group of peoples in Europe, many of whom (like the Roman, French and British aristocracies) chose at times to believe that they were descended from the Trojans. But it could (like 'tribe' and 'nation' and 'people') be extended to cover any set of humans, or animals. The expression 'the human race' is simply equivalent to 'human beings' or to *'homo sapiens'*. 'Race' is now somewhat tainted by undertones of 'racialism' or 'racism', the theory that moral and intellectual qualities (and especially inferiorities and superiorities) are genetically determined by racial membership. This purely political meaning dates from the nineteenth century and it is usually at variance with anthropological use.[1] Anti-semitism, for example, is a racialist doctrine, though the Jews do not constitute an ethnologically distinct race. 'Race' has come primarily to be associated with the doctrine of Nordic superiority over the Latins, and indeed over any dark-skinned peoples at all.

All the words in the verbal family I am considering have been taken over by political writers; the fate of 'race' is the least enviable. 'Nation', on the other hand, has been more fortunate. It too began as a serviceable term, in many contexts, for a group of people, and it long retained its synonymy with 'tribe', 'people' and 'race'. The *Oxford English Dictionary* cites Ben Jonson's *Sejanus*: 'You are a subtle nation, you physicians!' The word also had a technical usage in dividing up medieval universities. The University of Aberdeen contained the four nations of Mar, Buchan, Murray and Angus; whilst that of Paris was composed of the nations of France, Picardie, Normandie and Germany.

But already by the seventeenth century, especially in France and Germany, 'nation' was coming to stand for the political people of a society. Even as late as the early nineteenth century, a writer—a somewhat eccentric one—like Joseph de Maistre will define the nation as 'the king and the nobility'. The French nobility had long regarded themselves as racially and morally distinct from the rest of the French population. They alone were the 'nation'. This exclusiveness meant that the term 'nation' signified a club which everyone was anxious to join. On most views the decisive move came in the eighteenth century. To quote E. H. Carr, 'The founder of modern nationalism as it began to take shape in the nineteenth century was Rousseau, who, rejecting the embodiment of the nation in the personal sovereign or the ruling class, boldly identified "nation" and "people"; and this identification became a fundamental principle both of the French and of the American revolutions.'[2] For the 'people' to become the 'nation' was of course a promotion—one which we shall examine more closely in the next chapter.

'Nation' seemed further a more single and unified idea than 'people', even though 'people' in the eighteenth century did not always carry its later connotation of 'the masses' or 'the lower orders'. It retained an abstract reference to those of common birth who might be described as the 'stock'. Further, in its French context, 'nation' referred to a public interest, which contrasted favourably with the tangle of special private privileges which made up the *ancien régime*. The nation *was* the interests of everyone, by contrast with the plurality of classes, regions, corporations and perhaps religions which the state might contain. Given this powerful cluster of widely diffused ideas, we need not stress such accidents as that, in both English and French, the term 'state' has no acceptable adjectives. Hence it is that the French Deputies meet in the *Assemblée Nationale* whilst Britain groans under the burden of a 'National' Debt; certainly 'static debt' would be a highly misleading description, and not merely because 'state' and 'static' have different etymologies.

The respective destinies of 'state' and 'nation' are excellent illustrations of the place of persuasive emotional overtones in politics. For the 'state' was obviously political and closely associated with the overwhelming power so distrusted by liberals. Whole generations of men fought and schemed in order to reduce to a manageable level the arbitrary power of 'the state'. Later, Marxists described it as the 'executive committee of the bourgeois class' and looked forward to the time when it would wither away. And yet the obvious paradox of recent history has been the enormous growth of state power. How has this come about? It has been managed by politicians who claimed that the state was merely the executive of 'the nation'. With the growth of popular participation in politics, 'the nation' arose as a kind of gold-backing for the paper legislation issued by 'the state'. The 'state' might be 'them', but the 'nation' was 'us'.[3]

I shall not, now or later, attempt anything as exact as a definition of 'the nation'. But what one can say with confidence is that most nationalists have demanded that the nation should have some kind of pre-political unity. This unity might be that of religious belief, language, blood, or agreement on values and customs. Anything would do; and the more of this pre-political homogeneity, the better. And for the most part, the unchosen (like community of blood) was to be preferred to what at least in principle is a matter of choice (like religion). Renan's conclusion that the nation was ultimately based upon will was, in nationalist terms, a definitional defeat. Far more satisfactory in nationalist terms is Maurras's view, quoted by Professor Kedourie, 'that no Jew, no Semite, could understand or handle the French language as well as a Frenchman proper; no Jew, he remarked, could appreciate the beauties of Racine's line in *Bérénice: "Dans l'orient désert quel devint mon ennui"*.'[4] Nationalist doctrine usually argues that the state is based upon consent, but that the basis of the nation must be that it is a *natural* community.

The points at issue here are not merely verbal. The fate of words is frequently an accurate reflection of how people feel about themselves and the world they live in. Each word stands for a cluster of thoughts and sentiments which in each culture dissolve and recombine. Further, in politics definitions affect people's destinies. In the organisation of the Turkish nation after 1920, the Kurds proved a recalcitrant element. Mustapha Kemal dealt with this problem in a characteristically decisive way by deportation. But in the end, he shelved the problem verbally. The Kurds of Turkey were simply redescribed as 'mountain Turks'.[5]

The Classification of Nationalism

Every human being, whether he be Lapp or Laotian, Finn or French-man, belongs to some group with a collective name, and these names *can* all be seen as nationalities. But they need not be, and most people until quite recent times have been quite lacking in this sort of aware-ness. They have preferred to identify themselves by religion, allegiance to a monarch, city, locality, race or colour, rather than by nation. Let us then inspect those cases where national feeling has, by general agreement, been present.

First, in our inspection, we must consider the 'originals'—France perhaps, certainly Italy, Germany and Hungary: European peoples who strove to establish states which would incorporate all the members of the nation within one sovereign state. France is an ambiguous case, because France was in many ways their model. Nationalists sought to achieve what France (and Britain) already had. The classic situation was that a nation already existed, fragmented into a variety of states and principalities. Nationalism was an attempt to make the boundaries of the state and those of the nation coincide. It rapidly spread to all the other potential nationalities of Europe, so that for a time the whole continent seemed to think itself writhing in oppression. The Austro-Hungarian and Ottoman empires were the seed-beds of many nations. But whereas Italy and Germany had been large and more or less homogeneous communities (though even today, from Sicily to Lombardy is like moving to a foreign country), their imitators were interwoven in a demographic fabric which only violence and mass migration could even begin to unravel. Professor Trevor-Roper calls these peoples (Jews, Croats, Czechs, etc.) 'secondary nationalisms' by contrast with the 'historic nationalisms' of Germany, Italy and Hungary.[6] The Treaty of Versailles in 1919 made a heroic attempt to separate them out and succeeded only in demonstrating that the classic theory of nationalism was in their case a disastrous impossibility.

Next in our inspection, we may turn to the Afro-Asian world, which has since 1947 supplied dozens of states aspiring to full nationhood in the world political community. Most of these countries spent some time under the domination of one or other of the great

European empires. In discussing nationalism, we may class them together, and this classification is rendered plausible by the fact that most of them are 'underdeveloped'. But we must not lose sight of the fact that in nearly everything else—religion, language, technology, customs and way of life—they share little but their sheer variety. India is not typical, but it is in many ways a model of their development. India spent two centuries under British rule (compared with much less than a century for most African states). It contains hundreds of millions of people. It developed a varied and ingenious nationalist movement from about 1880 onwards and became a secular state in 1947. Contrast this with, say, Mauretania, inhabited by less than half a million mostly nomadic tribesmen. In Africa, political boundaries were drawn up by European statesmen, and they cut across tribal and ethnic boundaries with a fine disregard for all the foundations of nationalism. It is said that Germany at the time of the French Revolution was split up into about 350 states; but at least most of their inhabitants spoke German. Modern Nigeria's 55 million inhabitants are estimated to speak nearly 400 distinct languages. Will, not nature, must create such nations.

Next, consider a kind of nationalism which is often called a pan-movement; in the African context it is called macro-nationalism. These movements are distinguished by the fact that the nation in question is more than usually scattered and diffuse. Their early models were pan-Germanism and pan-Slavism. They have about them a visionary flavour and they have all so far proved to be failures, sometimes disastrously so. In our days, it is the pan-African movement which claims most of the headlines, and here the nation is an imprecise aspiration based upon geography and colour. As with most pan-movements, the imprecision of pan-Africanism results from uncertainty about what the macro-nation includes: is it merely the negro population south of the Sahara, or does it include the Arabs of the Mediterranean littoral? Does it include the Berbers, and the whites? On the other side of the world, Dr Sukarno in his days of power promoted a state called Maphilindo which would have combined Indonesia, Malaysia and the Philippines. This adumbration of a state amounts to a pan-Malay movement. It is hardly a strong popular movement, being largely the cerebral creation of Dr Sukarno

himself, but it does have a certain cultural and political plausibility
which might give it a future. Consider again the pan-Turanian movement which grew up before the First World War as a successor to
pan-Ottomanism and attracted the support of the foremost Turkish
nationalist of his day, Ziya Gökalp. Pan-Turanianism called for the
unification into one state of the entire linguistic and racial stock to
which the Turks belonged. Since the Turanians had migrated over
hundreds of years from the interior of Mongolia to the gates of
Vienna, they had covered a lot of ground, and left a lot of people
behind them. These peoples include the Uzbeks, the Kazaks and
various other of the smaller nationalities ruled since the nineteenth
century from Moscow. This, perhaps unlikely, aspiration had
sufficient grip upon the 'Young Turk' generation to induce Enver
Pasha in 1914 to lead the flower of the Turkish army towards the
Caucasus (and also towards disaster) in the hope of achieving some
of its aims. Indeed, such pan-Turanian calculations were among the
factors which in 1914 made Turkey so decisively a belligerent enemy
of Russia, and consequently an ally of Germany.[7]

Among the most active of these pan-movements today is the pan-
Arab, which dominates Middle Eastern politics. Pan-Arab aspirations
have led President Nasser of Egypt into temporary union with Syria;
they have involved him in civil war in the Yemen. Every political
upheaval in the Middle East must be reconciled at least with the
rhetoric of pan-Arabism. Like all pan-movements, the envisaged
boundaries of the final state are subject to alternating moods of
ambition and realism: it is a disputed question, for example, whether
the Maghrib should be part of a pan-Arab state.

Pan-movements have at one time or another been thought to
encompass the entire population of the world. There has been
occasional support for a pan-Latin union in Europe. And there have
been many political forms of a movement one might call pan-Anglo-
Saxondom. When Joseph Chamberlain said in Toronto in 1887: 'I
refuse to speak or to think of the United States as a foreign nation',
he was expressing the most ambitious of the many schemes of that
period for a Greater Britain which should incorporate 'the young and
vigorous nations carrying everywhere a knowledge of the English
tongue and English love of liberty and law'.[8] These movements

might be called racialist; they were in fact at the time called imperialist. But what they amount to is summed up in the title of Seeley's famous lectures on 'the Expansion of England', and this was often conceived in national terms. In another form these aspirations acquired a religious premise. The British Israelites believed that the English were descended from the Lost Tribes of Israel, and were therefore God's chosen people. And in later times, there have been projects for 'union now' between the United States and the British Dominions. Here, as with all pan-movements, the primary impulse seems to be a form of Great Power dreaming, for the political union of these cultural and racial families would in all cases produce a formidable new actor on the international stage. Political domination is prominent among the advantages suggested for such unions.

Next we may mention the nationalism of people in search of a home. The two instances of this class that spring immediately to mind are Zionism and its imitator among American Negroes called the Black Muslim movement. The nationalism of the homeless is a good example of the effect of nationalist ideas. Both the Jews in Europe and the Negroes in America belong to social minorities which have suffered various forms of discrimination. The concentration camps on the one hand, cases of lynch law on the other, are merely the extremes of oppression which merges into pettifogging harassment. There have always been groups suffering in this way—witness the Untouchables of India. But it takes the influence of nationalist theory to convince such sufferers, firstly, that they are a nation (for the Jews are in the first instance a religious community, the Negroes a racial category drawn from many sources) and, secondly, that the solution is to find a territorial home and establish a state. These two cases of homeless nationalism are spectacular because the European Zionist found his home in far-off Israel, and projects for an African home ranged from Canada to the partial application of the idea in Liberia. But this kind of homelessness is in many ways similar to, say, that of the Kurds who have been fighting the Iraqi government throughout the 1960s to establish a home of their own, an independent Kurdistan. But being actually on the spot assimilates the Kurds to the sort of European nationalism we have already discussed.

And lastly, within this group, we might include fascism or totalitarian nationalism. It is an open question whether totalitarian nationalism is a proper form of nationalism at all; but it is certainly true that writers in the 1930s and 40s often did not hesitate to see in the careers of Hitler and Mussolini, not to mention their many less spectacular imitators, the culmination of nationalist folly. It is further true that if we were to take nationalist rhetoric seriously, we should have to conclude that it seems to be demanding the conditions of a totalitarian state in which nothing is in principle taken as private and beyond political regulation in the interest of the nation.

Our inspection is ended. We need not pursue the finer points of how we might mark off nationalism from other political phenomena. In fact, for many writers, there are no such borders. Every set of barefoot guerrillas hiding out in the jungle with rusty rifles is a nationalist movement, and every casual use of nationalist rhetoric is evidence of its ubiquity. The very word 'nationalism' has the power of stopping thought. This may be illustrated, not from those who comment on current affairs, but from thoughtful writers with a sound grasp of the history of nationalism. When for example we find C. M. Woodhouse writing: 'Every revolution in Syria since independence, which means roughly once every two years on average since the Second World War, has been a nationalist revolution',[9] we would be wise to pause and look closer. On 30 March 1949 the General Command of the Army issued a statement saying: 'Today a new page has been turned in the life of the Arab people of Syria; other pages have been closed. The page turned is one of heroism and glory; the closed ones are of humiliation and disgrace.' Following the second *coup d'état* of 14 August 1949, Brigadier Sami al-Hinnawi issued a statement saying: 'Praise God, the Sublime and Almighty, the real *coup d'état* has been accomplished, and the country has been saved from the criminal and despotic tyrant who had deviated from the proper course and who had ruled most despotically. . . .'[10] Now while it is probably true that some issues of Arab nationalism were affected by each *coup d'état* in turn, it is also true that not even the official gloss on these political upheavals claimed an entirely nationalist inspiration. It is almost a law of nationalist politics that if nationalist slogans *can* be used, they *will* be. The upheavals in Syria are like most political upheavals caused by factional struggles in which ideological issues may well play quite a small part.

Normally, the vaguer statements of the literature are difficult to pin down by virtue of their very ambiguity. But one moderately precise issue worth considering is when writers come to discuss the moment when nationalism came into the world.

Arnold Toynbee writes that it was in 1775 that 'the principle of nationality first asserted itself in the modern world as a dynamic political force'.[11] Or Professor Hans Kohn: 'Modern nationalism originated in the seventeenth and eighteenth centuries in north-west Europe and its American settlements. . . . It became a general European movement in the nineteenth century.'[12] Professor Snyder tells us that 'modern nationalism may be dated from 1688, 1770 and 1789'.[13] Professor Kedourie begins his account of nationalism: 'Nationalism is a doctrine invented in Europe at the beginning of the nineteenth century.'[14] In his recent study of fascism, Professor Nolte tells us that 'the defeat at Adowa in 1896 . . . kindled the beginnings of nationalism (in Italy), even if at first this occurred more in the minds of individual men . . . than in the visible form of publications or organisations.'[15] Meanwhile we find Sir Steven Runciman talking of Bulgar nationalism in the Middle Ages,[16] and Professor Tout in generalising mood has written: 'The history of modern Europe is the history of the development of nationalities. That history may be said in a sense to begin with the establishment of the first of an unbroken dynasty of national kings over what was destined to become one of the greatest of modern nations.'[17] (He is writing of Hugh Capet in France.)

If we take them literally, these statements contradict each other. If we look to the context, we shall find that most of them can be justified—but only if we recognise that each statement is referring to a different thing. This is a problem which torments anyone writing of nationalism, for while such expressions as 'nationalism', 'the principle of nationality' and 'modern nationalism' may stand for different things, there is a good deal of fuzziness at the margins. This chapter is largely concerned to sort out this problem. Let us conclude this section by indicating several ways in which the field has been carved up.

First we may distinguish between the body of political writing—the doctrine, the ideology, the rhetoric—and on the other hand, the political movement or sentiment taken to determine political events. Professor Kedourie, for example, was in the passage we quoted talking about nationalist doctrine, and his dating of the emergence of these ideas would command general acceptance. He goes on immediately to circumscribe this literature closely: 'It pretends to supply a criterion for the determination of the unity of population proper to enjoy a government exclusively its own, for the legitimate exercise of power in the state, and for the right organisation of a society of states.' Once we move beyond the doctrine, we are in a much vaguer area.

Next, we might mention the attempt to order nationalism by distinguishing the *area* of life in which it operates. When writers think in this way we find accounts of cultural nationalism, religious nationalism, linguistic nationalism, or economic nationalism. This is a distinction worth keeping in mind, because nationalism is in fact unpredictable in its invasions of different areas of social life. Wales, for example, has a strong and extensive cultural nationalism, whilst its political wing (*Plaid Cymru*) was for a long time politically ineffective.

Lastly we might mention the attempt to characterise the *kind* of nationalist politics we encounter: and in these terms, we find liberal, conservative, integral, right-wing and left-wing nationalisms distinguished. People thinking in these terms are likely to ask such questions as: Is nationalism fundamentally a radical or a conservative force? I am inclined to think that this is a misleading way of regarding the subject. For these distinctions suggest the illusory possibility that we may be able to find some ideological connection between nationalism and kinds of politics. It has commonly been thought, for example, that nationalism is—fundamentally or 'by nature'—a right-wing phenomenon, and that where we find nationalism combined with left-wing attitudes, some additional explanation is required. These are lines of inquiry likely to be suggested to anyone who has been touched by the Marxist view that nationalism is generally one stage of the development of the bourgeois state.

It seems to me that to pursue this line of inquiry would lead only to wasted ingenuity. For to describe the politics of any country as nationalist is to say that its politics are dominated by a particular *issue*. We may specify this issue abstractly as the defence of national values. Now the content of the values, and the development of the issue, is entirely determined by the situation of the country. We cannot say in advance, without looking to the particular culture, what the content will be. It might seem, for example, that nationalism (which demands national unity) is *a priori* hostile to a socialism which asserts that bourgeoisie and proletariat inevitably conflict. But some Arab nationalists have solved this difficulty by questioning whether the bourgeoisie is part of the Arab nation. We might expect communist states to be free of nationalism, since Marxists condemn it as a bourgeois doctrine. But we would be wrong. There appears to be no major ideology of the modern world with which nationalism is entirely incompatible. Let us now turn from the analysis of nationalism to its history.

The Received View of Nationalism

Thousands of books have been written about nationalism; most tell a similar story. It is a kind of philosophy of European history. With a brisk glance backwards to the Jews and the Greeks of the ancient world, writers tend to exhibit nationalism emerging from the decline of feudal Europe. Like the bourgeoisie, nationalism is one of those things that always seems to be growing. It may be found growing amidst the incidents of the Hundred Years War between the Valois and Plantagenet monarchs with their capitals in Paris and London. It may be seen in the sense of mission developed by the kings of Castile as they prosecuted against the Muslims the wars known as the *reconquista*. It has often been detected in the feelings of support some Germans felt for their Emperor in his periodic clashes with the Pope. But these medieval examples are shadowy. The historian of nationalism (who is usually also its analyst) is happier when he moves on to the chapter called 'the growth of the nation-state'. Here the histories of France, Spain and England (along with Holland and Portugal) are told in terms of the activities of centralising monarchs. And it is certainly true that acute contemporaries then had a stronger sense that something new was happening. Machiavelli, for example, looked with envy at new European states which could fight wars without recourse to mercenaries. The religious fragmentation of the sixteenth century fits well into this story. Luther on the one hand, the Anglican church on the other look like the religious strand in the fabric of state-centralisation. And from state-centralisation—the thread which nearly all historians use to guide themselves through the maze of these centuries—it is a small step to nation-state-centralisation.

In terms of these major abstractions, the story then faces something of a gap from roughly 1650 to 1750. The gap can be bridged by an account of the expansionist wars of Louis XIV; by Milton's notion that God regarded the English as his chosen people; and perhaps by the patriotic notions of Bolingbroke. During this period the principle of nationality seemed to have received a check: static entirely in Germany and Italy and perhaps even retrogressing in Spain. Cosmopolitanism was rampant and wars aristocratic.

From the middle of the eighteenth century, the story warms up, never to grow cold again. The American War of Independence is sometimes cited as a triumph of national consciousness. The drift of France into Revolution is the point where at last firm ground has been reached, for we arrive finally at explicit and conscious use of the terms 'nation' and 'nationalism'. Here we begin to find a fuller justification for such typically presiding utterances as: 'Nationalism has been, indeed, the chief motivating ideal of political development throughout the modern era . . . the whole trend of modern history has been towards the development and the culmination in the twentieth century, of nationalism as a political theory and a political fact.'[18] Or: 'As a historic force nationalism has been a major factor uninterruptedly since the French Revolution.'[19] Besides, it is from this point on that the writer has available the writings of that joker in any cultural-history pack, Jean-Jacques Rousseau, whose ambiguous words and conflicting emotions supply evidence for many varied strands of history.

In the nineteenth century, the problem of telling the story is simply *embarras de richesse*. Italy and Germany are the indispensable characters, and quotations from Fichte may jostle alongside accounts of Garibaldi and his thousand redshirts toppling the kingdom of Naples. Eastern Europe especially presents a picture of the Hapsburg and Ottoman empires seething with suppressed nationalities. The story is at this point further enriched by a plentiful supply of mass movements intersecting with nationalism, either as cause or consequence. This is the moment of triumph, and also of a change of tone. It is difficult to keep the strands of the story apart, and one solution is to jumble them up together and face the resulting contradictions squarely: ' . . . nationalism is full of ambivalence. It is on the one hand a conservative force, but on the other hand a revolutionary factor.'[20] From Mazzini's vision of liberty and peace as the fruits we might pluck from national liberation, the historian is forced onward to the more sinister developments of late-nineteenth-century nationalism. He must tell of European nations scrambling to carve out empires for themselves throughout the world, and especially in Africa. And he must tell of mounting suspicion and recrimination leading to the arms race that continued up to 1914.

After the First World War both the tone and the content of the story change. Beauty has now unmistakably turned monstrous. Nationalism seems now to be at its most intense, and also at its nastiest. It is easy to see European history from 1918 to 1939, when dictatorship seemed to be the preferred principle of government, as a time of morbid and aggravated nationalism. The Second World War can be as easily assimilated to the nationalist story as the First. Few writers can resist expressing their horror at this culmination, and most reveal their hopes. 'That the traditional nation-state is obsolescent in view of the technological and military conditions of the contemporary world is obvious', writes Professor Morgenthau. 'Yet, while trying to replace it with a larger unit, better attuned to these conditions, it is well to take care that it be not replaced simply by a more efficient vehicle for the crusading nationalism of our age.'[21] But is it obvious that the nation-state is obsolescent? Here the wish is father to the thought, and historical distortion comes to be produced as much by internationalist aspirations as by nationalist bias.

Nationalism has now spread all over the world. In Africa, Asia and Latin America, the area in other contexts described as 'underdeveloped', politics presents us with an image of masses on the move.

If we ask what electricity it is that moves so many different men in so many different places, the simplest answer, the one that allows us to stop thinking most comfortably, is: Nationalism. And again the storyteller's problem is that there is so much to tell. Either he concentrates on a few examples, or his story is an almost incomprehensible conglomerate of towns, battles, declarations, meetings and dates. A history always limited to the bones has become so skeletal as to reach disappearing point.

Such is the historical material with which any writer on nationalism is called on to deal. And the obvious objection is that nationalism as an idea has grown so big that it has absorbed most of European history. In philosophy, as in economics, there is a law of diminishing returns which tells us that the wider a concept is stretched the less meaningful it becomes. Our appreciation of this law is, in the case of nationalism, enhanced by the high cliché-content of many tellings of this story. But let us particularise, and consider a point which exemplifies the dangers of the received story.

There is a fact about nationalism which has struck many disparate observers. Here, for example, is John Maynard Keynes describing Clemenceau at the Versailles peace conference of 1919: 'He felt about France what Pericles felt of Athens—unique value in her, nothing else mattering; but his theory of politics was Bismarck's. He had one illusion—France; and one disillusion—mankind, including Frenchmen, and his colleagues not least. . . . His philosophy had, therefore, no place for "sentimentality" in international relations. Nations are real things, of whom you love one and feel for the rest indifference —or hatred. The glory of the nation you love is a desirable end—but generally to be obtained at your neighbour's expense.'[22] Or again consider the remark General Beck is reported to have made about Hitler: 'This fellow has no Fatherland at all.'[23] This casual remark made in the 1930s was to be illustrated in a grim manner by the way in which the Hitler of the Berlin bunker railed against the German people as unworthy of him. Or consider another example. Here are words attributed to Michael Collins, an Irish nationalist leader. 'I stand for an Irish civilisation based on the people and embodying and maintaining the things—their habits, ways of thought, customs —that make them different—the sort of life I was brought up in. . . .

Once, years ago, a crowd of us were going along the Shepherd's Bush Road when out of a lane came a chap with a donkey—just the sort of donkey and just the sort of cart that they have at home. He came out quite suddenly and abruptly and we all cheered him. Nobody who has not been an exile will understand me, but I stand for that.'[24] But there is a gap between this image of Irish life on the one hand, and revolutionary and terrorist activity on the other. It is the usual gap between any act and its justification, and logic will not bridge it.

Lastly, consider the case of Charles Maurras: monarchist, nationalist, fascist, he was a stalwart of the *Action Française* for half a century. Although he used nationalist slogans (such as *la France d'abord*) Maurras found himself in increasing difficulties in the 1930s. He supported the Spanish rebellion which led to the victory of General Franco; supported, in other words, a potential enemy of France in circumstances when she was already threatened by Germany. And even his opposition to Germany became half-hearted. In his youth he had diagnosed the German obsession with 'I' as the reason why she had become so dangerous a nation to France, and he had interpreted German resistance to Napoleon as a kind of 'revolt of the slaves'. Yet during the war he collaborated with the Germans, and his anti-Semitism, once so intellectually distinguished from the more vulgar varieties, outstripped that of the Germans.[25]

Common to all these examples is a certain intellectualisation of the idea of the nation concerned. Nationalism, in other words, appears to be a love for an abstraction of the nation, and that abstraction may have none but the most tenuous connection with the concrete national life. Clemenceau loving France and rather disliking Frenchmen expresses this paradox of nationalism. What we find, in fact, is involvement in a fantasy, and those involved in a fantasy are liable to violent and unpredictable rage if the world fails to fit their dreams. Why this should be so is perhaps difficult to understand in depth. One suggestive fact (explicit here in the case of Collins) is that exile is a common experience of nationalists, especially the leaders of developing nations, most of whom have gone abroad for part of their education. It is a common observation that many nationalist leaders come from the periphery of their countries. One is, indeed, tempted to generalise the idea of exile, and regard modern nationalism as a recourse of those who feel spiritually exiled from their communities: the outsiders, the alienated, the excluded.

The point of this excursion into the psychology of nationalism is to demonstrate that what looks like a patriotic love of country may in fact have nothing more to do with it than the use of rhetorical phrases. Nationalism, far from being similar to patriotism, often comes very close to being its opposite: they may well be distinguished as love of quite different things. The fact that those two things may have the same name ('France' or 'Germany') should not be allowed to confuse us, for in succumbing to that confusion we stumble into the role of nationalist ideologists. And this we do whenever we transform expressions of patriotic sentiment either into nationalism itself or some sort of precursor. The army whose heart was stirred by Queen Elizabeth I speaking at Tilbury of her determination to resist the Spanish Armada were no doubt patriotic, but they responded to a personal loyalty to the Queen, and to a sense that the realm was in danger: ' . . . I am come amongst you, as you see, at this time, not for my recreation and disport, but being resolved, in the midst and heat of the battle, to live or die amongst you all, to lay down for my God, and for my kingdom, and for my people, my honour and my blood, even in the dust. I know I have the body of a weak and feeble woman, but I have the heart and stomach of a king, and of a king of England too, and think foul scorn that Parma or Spain or any prince of Europe should dare to invade the borders of my realm; to which, rather than any dishonour shall grow by me, I myself will take up arms, I myself will be your general, judge, and rewarder of every one of your virtues in the field.' This is patriotism, not nationalism. It will not even do to suggest that Elizabeth's subjects experienced 'national feeling' or 'national consciousness', for while they may have felt loyalty to something they called 'England', they did not go on to take the next essential step, which is to call England a nation, with all that such an expression means to us today. It is no doubt true that patriotism was one of the roots from which the strength of nationalism grew; but until late in the eighteenth century, this modern modification, indeed transformation, of patriotic feelings was quite unpredictable.

We face here a conflict of interests. It is the business of the ideologist of nationalism to persuade us that history culminates in nationalism. In a similar way, Marxists force history on to the Procrustes' bed of the class struggle, and Christians are sometimes disposed to see the hand of Providence everywhere. Ideologists, like egoists, see little else but their own reflection, and it is part of their strength that they should do so.

Our business, by contrast, is to disentangle ourselves from these confusions, to prevent history from being put through the mangle of nationalist ideology, to stand aside from nationalist legend. For many reasons (among them, the enthusiasm of students who see the subject they study everywhere they look) the received story of nationalism is radically infected by confusions: as in the case of the classification of nationalism, the study *of* the ideology has been infected *by* the ideology.

Three Stages of Nationalism

Nationalism is a political movement which seeks to attain and defend an objective we may call national integrity. It seeks 'freedom', but freedom can mean many things. The demand for freedom already carries with it the suggestion that nationalists feel themselves oppressed. Out of this freedom–oppression complex of ideas we may extract a general description of nationalism: it is a political movement depending on a feeling of collective grievance against foreigners.

The nationalist grievance must be collective. And the collectivity must be the nation. Irish peasants and gentry felt all manner of grievances against English rule for centuries, but they felt these grievances as an oppressed class, or religious community, or locality. It took the winds of nationalism blowing from the Continent to provide a new understanding of the Irish situation. Nationalism not merely gives an intellectual status to the grievance, it also adds items to it. Most human beings have always been governed by foreigners; many have indeed found that the very fact of foreignness means that their rulers are agreeably impartial when judging local disputes. But nationalism teaches that the fact of foreign rule itself is an affront to human dignity.

Further, this teaching has a singular power of organising vague feelings of discontent into something more political. Faced with any block to their desires, people acquainted with nationalist ideas feel that they understand why they are unhappy. This singular quality of organising grievances is common to all powerful modern ideologies.

The grievance must be caused by foreigners. Nationalism need not in fact involve xenophobia, and nationalism is often directed quite explicitly against a foreign government, combined with the insistence that 'we have no quarrel with the British, French, German, etc., people'. The point here is that nationalism cannot be *purely* a struggle of internal factions within a country. Yet in the looking-glass world of modern politics, 'foreigner' can include 'agent of a foreign power' or 'imperialist agent'. Thus Nuri Said, prime minister of Iraq until 1958, spent most of his life propagating the doctrine of Arab nationalism, and was in the end struck down by those who accused him of servitude to British interests.[26] Hence there is a special nationalist category of 'traitors' or 'honorary foreigners'. The commonest 'honorary foreigners' have been Jews, whose catastrophic role as a kind of nationalist litmus paper is one of the most tragic stories of the twentieth century. But the rich will do just as well, if nationalism gets entangled with socialism; or, conversely, though less commonly, the poor may get suspected of disloyalty.

If we identify nationalism in this way, then it will be clear that it is a three-stage process and that each stage is in principle clearly distinguishable. Reality, of course, is much less tidy.

The first stage may be loosely labelled *stirrings*. This is the period in which the nation becomes aware of itself as a nation suffering oppression. Frequently it is a period of revulsion against foreign ideas and foreign ways of doing things. It is a time of casting around for a cultural identity. It is likely, for example, that a religion which was abandoned in the first flush of enthusiasm for foreign ideas will be revived. The country which best exemplifies the model I am describing is India, and here the time of stirrings included a revival of Hinduism in which many elements hitherto taken laxly (such as the sacredness of the cow) became far more rigid. There is, of course, something artificial about this kind of religious revival, since a nationalist espousal of Hinduism turns it into one element of national self-definition. It was never that before. In the case of Germany, which counts as a pioneer of nationalist theory, this period produced theories of cultural autonomy and rejection of cosmopolitanism. The work of the brothers Grimm, who developed the philology of the German language and collected folk tales, illustrates the fact that this is a time when intellectuals develop the nationalist movement. Much of this work is, of course, of genuine intellectual value, but its direction is vulnerable to political pressure. African nationalists, for example, are eager to discover fragments of lost civilisations which will supply Africans with glorious forebears. In fact, of course, the worth of Africans does not, and could not possibly, depend upon the findings of these researches; but the drive of nationalist theory is to discover a past which will support the aspiration of the present. In other words, this is the stage of legend-making.

The material for these legends is the entire history of the community in question. The connections may well be tenuous in the extreme. Many Africans have felt a thrill of pride at the achievements of Hannibal. They have identified Africa with the glories of ancient Egypt. Nationalists will turn every patriotic event into a piece of nationalist legend; in this way they transform history and introduce the sort of distortions we discussed in the last section. Further, this may involve a certain amount of renaming. Indian nationalists, for example, are inclined to turn that event which English textbooks call the 'Indian Mutiny' into the First War of Indian Independence.

The second stage is the centrepiece of nationalism: it is the time of the *struggle* for independence. The struggle may or may not have an obvious moment of beginning, but it usually has a fixed terminus. Since 1945 that fixed terminus has been the attainment of sovereign independence and admission to the United Nations. For Italy, it was perhaps Victor Emmanuel's entry into Rome in 1861; for Germany, the signing of peace with France in the hall of mirrors at Versailles in 1871. The actual content of the struggle varies enormously. It may involve terrorism, or full-scale guerrilla warfare. Or there may be riots and demonstrations. Or the work of struggle may simply be a continual process of peaceful political negotiation. But again, the vital thing is that it should provide a legend of heroes backed up by the resilience of national virtues. But this stage is vital for national self-respect.

It is so vital, indeed, that where it does not exist it may have to be invented. In the later stages of decolonisation, the European empires were liquidating their colonial heritage so fast that in many cases there was no serious resistance whatsoever. An articulate group of national politicians had merely to present themselves on the political stage and negotiations would begin on the transfer of power. Such has been the case with most of the African states which became independent around 1960. How much they have needed to build up a legend of struggle, or a sense of continuing threats to independence, has been a function of variable internal politics. Again, some nationalists have believed that the ideal way of arriving at national statehood is by way of a moderately difficult military struggle which will draw everyone into it and develop a corps of leaders who can take over later on. But the danger of this—as the case of Algeria illustrates—is that the war may well exhaust national resources.

We may call the third stage of the process *consolidation*. Sometimes this stage hardly exists at all. India after 1947, for example, moved straight on to the ordinary preoccupations of a state—economic development and sustaining a foreign policy. Nationalist issues as such have played comparatively little part in Indian politics since independence. There were, of course, times when nationalist emotions might be used, as in the taking of the Portuguese enclave of Goa. But the dispute with Pakistan over Kashmir, or that with China in the Himalayas, is not specifically linked to nationalism. Indonesia, on the other hand, is an example of a case where the period of consolidation went on for years, in the form of the claim for West Irian, and the 'confrontation' with Malaysia. These were precisely nationalist disputes, and they were used for a specifically nationalist purpose—maintaining national unity and warding off the transition to other kinds of politics.

For the most obvious feature of nationalism in the Afro–Asian world is that very often there is no nation at all. The complex of peoples, races and religions which make up many such countries gains virtually the only unity to which it may lay claim from the struggle for independence. Arrived at independence, such countries are in danger of falling apart. The continuation of a nationalist struggle then becomes an ingenious device for ruling a realm which has been persuaded by nationalist rhetoric that homogeneity is essential to a state, and which does not in fact possess it. Here then is the reason why the day after independence, leaders of new states are to be found proclaiming that the struggle has not ended, but has only entered a new phase. The notion that politics is a struggle is one heritage of nationalism—struggle is to a nationalist what thrift is to a puritan, something which purports to be done for a reason, but which in fact sums up a complete understanding of life. In addition, of course, there are always unsophisticated nationalists who have come to believe that *all* problems derive from the fact that the nation is oppressed. They have been encouraged in this very belief by nationalist rhetoric, and they may therefore be deeply shocked to discover that poverty and disagreement continue to be features of national life.

In recent years, the period of consolidation has come increasingly to be seen in economic terms. The nation, it is believed, can only be consolidated once it has become a developed economy. This is a belief which projects the consolidation into an almost endless future, for the concept of a 'developed' economy is determined by what happens in the most economically advanced areas of the world. But this shift of emphasis is one way in which nationalist theory is likely to liquidate itself and shunt the energies of men into the more familiar paths of economic development.

The notion of nationalism as a collective grievance against foreigners, and its analysis into three stages, may be extracted from an examination of nationalist theory, and without very much reference to actual political experience. The point of this treatment is to limit the concept of nationalism to something distinctive in modern politics. On this view, it must be concluded that many nations have had relatively little nationalist experience. Britain and the United States, for example, have seldom had the kinds of grievance susceptible of nationalist politics. The American War of Independence does indeed fit into this kind of three-stage analysis, and it is very easy to see it in nationalist terms. Yet it would seem that the people of the American colonies, while they certainly developed a rapid awareness of themselves as Americans, did not think seriously of themselves as an American nation. Their struggle came too early for them to conduct it in that way. Again, in a very vague sense, one can talk of Australian nationalism—a growing sense of Australian specialness in the English-speaking world. There is even the material for a legend, in the form of a group of discontented gold-miners on the Ballarat goldfields who in 1851 built the Eureka Stockade and declared themselves the Republic of the Southern Cross. This was a genuinely nationalist experience, but it was remote from the circumstances of Australian life. Its only consequences were literary and legendary. Australian political development, from self-government through to federation of the Australian states in 1900, was uncomplicated by a struggle against the British government, and no serious body of political opinion ever thought it worth while to pretend that this was not the case. During the economic depression of the 1930s, the premier of New South Wales thought it worth while to raise the cry of oppression by foreign (i.e. British) bankers, but this appeal to the nationalist issue was unsuccessful.

The literature of nationalism is likely to class under this comprehensive name a collection of political facts which we can range in ascending order. First comes the kind of nationalist phenomenon we have just mentioned. It consists of currents of feeling—anti-Americanism in particular sections of many peoples since 1945 is a good example. There is always likely to be hostility towards powerful neighbours, and in modern times this hostility will be expressed in nationalist terms. Competitive feeling at such sporting events as the Olympic Games is another example of this kind of nationalist emotion. Further, many countries contain some local *führer* whose followers seek to exploit nationalist feeling. Such leaders are one of the permanent options of politics, and for a disastrous period after the First World War, the option was taken up in many countries. All of these things may legitimately enough be called nationalism, but they constitute a rag-bag without much intellectual coherence.

Next we may ascend to three-stage nationalism such as we have just described. The point here is that the nationalist *issue* has come to dominate the political development of the country. Nothing can be done without its being seen in nationalist terms.

Beyond that, we have what has often been called integral nationalism. Here lies totalitarianism, which often looks like an insanely detailed application of nationalist theory—as it did in the case of Nazism. It may well be (and it has been persuasively argued by such writers as Hannah Arendt and Ernst Nolte) that resemblances are superficial, and that totalitarianism is a quite different kind of political thing. But whether totalitarianism is distinguished from nationalism by quality or by degree need not here detain us; for our purposes, it may be left to one side.

If we treat the subject in this way, we need not break our heads over trying to define a 'nation'. Any single test of nationhood breaks down. In effect, each nationalist proposes as the critical test whatever is closest to his heart. For Spaniards, Catholicism, and for many Turks, Islam, is the key to the national soul; but since the secularisation of the state, many impeccable nations contain a plurality of religions. Others have taken purity of race; but humanity is genetically too scrambled for any such notion of national purity. Where this criterion is pushed to its limit, it becomes racialism, and (as in the case of the Nazis) the pure race comes to be a quite different set of people from the nation with which the racialist started. The most popular criterion has been language, the very mention of which provokes us to remember that the Swiss nation speaks four languages. Language has been important enough in some nationalisms to cause the revival or rediffusion of a language otherwise disappearing—as in the Irish attempt to revive Gaelic. Faced with the collapse of any single criterion, complex and abstract definitions have been suggested. Yet in a metaphorical sense, language remains the more promising candidate. A nation does consist of 'people who speak the same language'.

In our terms, there is no need to define a nation precisely, because once it exists, there will be little need to try. A nation as a living component of nationalism is something to be found largely in the aspirations of nationalists. It consists of all those people who have been persuaded that they share in the national grievance.

Finally in this introductory survey, let us anticipate Chapter 6 and ask why nationalism was born into the modern world. Can we find a general condition of things from which nationalism seems primordially to spring? Our clue may be that nationalism in both France and Germany became the spearhead of an attack upon feudalism. Outside Europe, we find many traditional societies in which custom is no longer an adequate guide to behaviour. Where the tradition has crumbled we usually find a rapid growth of population, much of it congregating in cities. We find a rapid shift to literacy. Women emerge from the hearth, and young people start behaving insolently and ignoring the advice of their fathers. New kinds of politician arise. It is a new world full of wonders. The image which appeals irresistibly to people in this condition is that of birth pangs, for their condition is both painful and hopeful. It is true, of course, that nationalism is not an inevitable answer to the problems posed. What is in process of birth may as easily be the city of God, or the Communist society, as the nation. The intellectual resources of Western civilisation have combed for a solution to the bafflement which this kind of social crisis induces. How can we explain the popularity of ideologies like nationalism?

The formula that I find most convincing is to say that nationalism provides an escape from triviality. Implicitly or explicitly, men suffering a social upheaval put to themselves the question: What is happening to us? The nationalist answer is clear: Our nation is struggling to be born; it is fighting for independence against its enemies. This answer is never the whole truth, and sometimes it has absolutely nothing to do with the truth at all. But that does not matter. The nationalist struggle is a noble one which dignifies a man's sufferings, and gives him a hopeful direction in which to work. When the Greek National Assembly in 1822 declared: 'We, descendants of the wise and noble peoples of Hellas . . . find it no longer possible to suffer without cowardice and self-contempt the cruel yoke of the Ottoman power which has weighed upon us for more than four centuries',[27] it expressed a sense of grandeur and a feeling of self-satisfaction little different from Patrice Lumumba in 1960: 'Of this struggle, one of tears, fire and blood, we are proud to the very depths of our being, for it was a noble and just struggle, absolutely necessary in order to bring to an end the humiliating slavery which had been imposed upon us by force.'[28]

2

Nationalism and
the French Revolution

Nationalism is a European invention. It is a new way in which men came to understand politics. But unlike many understandings of philosophers, this new view of things was a powerful weapon of political change. It could be explained easily to unsophisticated people, and it did become a vision to which many dedicated their lives. Nationalism is a river fed by many converging streams. Most of the streams are to be found—flowing in other directions—in eighteenth-century France. In this chapter we shall examine some of them.

Intellectual Life in Eighteenth-century France

Eighteenth-century Europe was cosmopolitan. The education of a man of means consisted in travelling abroad, and developing a rational urbanity about local custom. Philosophers thought in terms of reason and humanity. French had replaced Latin as the language of Christendom. The barometer seemed set fair for pacifist cosmopolitanism, but the rains came. Where, in such a milieu, do we find the seeds of nationalism? Bourbon France, wretchedly unsuccessful in imposing its military will upon the rest of Europe, had nonetheless arrived at a cultural hegemony as complete as that of Rome. The success of this hegemony arose not merely from the glories of French classicism and the elegant utility of the French language, but also from the gracious manner in which it was exercised. The *philosophes* were so liberated from parochial points of view that their more mischievous spirits could take on the mask of Persian, or Chinese, or of the South Sea Islands, and mock the unreflective follies of their fellow Europeans.

33

The absence of any narrow spirit of political competition is most clearly demonstrated in French Anglophilia of the period. Montesquieu took the British Constitution as a key which would unlock the problem of political liberty. Voltaire spent many polemical years championing the Newtonian system of cosmology against homegrown Cartesian vortices. The epistemology of Locke was hailed as a pronouncement of common sense which had put to flight all the misty systems of knowledge previously current. And the sheer intellectual autonomy of these events is revealed when we remember that for roughly half of the eighteenth century, Britain and France were at war. Never, it might seem, had culture and politics been kept so resolutely, and so happily, apart.

The French *philosophes* acted as a European clearing-house of critical ideas. They judged these ideas entirely in rational terms. They paid no attention to national origins. They created new institutions by which mankind could carry on a purely rational conversation—international correspondences, dictionaries, and especially, of course, the great Encyclopaedia. The principles and attitudes of enlightened liberalism may have been formed in the verbal dough of John Locke, but the *philosophes* supplied the yeast, and all Europe came to the banquet. What they contributed to liberalism was not simply a set of principles, often expressed in epigrams, but also a feeling of being the vanguard of human rationality, a spearhead probing the entrenched but doomed forces of superstition, vested interest, and parochiality.[1]

They were proud of being French, but proud in a generous manner quite lacking in the stridency of later nationalism. 'There was no reason to expect Frenchmen to distinguish themselves in philosophy', wrote Voltaire in the *Encyclopédie*. 'An extended period of gothic government extinguished all light for a period of almost twelve centuries; and teachers, riddled with error, paid to brutalise human nature, made the darkness yet darker: today however there is more philosophy in Paris than in any town on earth, and perhaps even than in all the towns put together, except for London.'[2] When Voltaire does claim virtues for the French, it is a claim to those virtues, accessible to all, which accompany a rational attitude of mind: 'The genius of this language is clarity and order.' In 1783 Rivarol, in a prize essay for the Berlin Academy, put this even more concisely in the slogan: 'If it isn't clear, it isn't French.'

The situation of the *philosophes* in France was unusual in a number of significant ways. De Tocqueville has described, in a famous chapter, how around the middle of the eighteenth century men of letters were also the principal political figures of the *ancien régime*.[3] What struck de Tocqueville particularly was the absolute split between the men exercising authority on the one hand, and those who dominated political discussion (which was ubiquitous) on the other. He contrasted this situation unfavourably with that of England at the same period. So too, of course, did many of the *philosophes* themselves. But whereas de Tocqueville regretted the gap between political life and literary theory because he believed it was bad for literature, the *philosophes* regretted more simply their lack of political power.

De Tocqueville remarks that the writers of the period supplied the people not only with opinions, but also with a temperament and a disposition. They diffused a pseudo-intellectuality and a disposition in favour of abstract arguments. And this he connects up with what seemed to him one of the strangest features of that period: that no one seems to have entertained the slightest desire for a violent revolution. He read through the great body of *Cahiers* composed by each of the Three Estates in 1789. 'I see that here someone demands the change of a law, there of a custom, and I make a note. I keep on to the end of this enormous labour, and when I come to put together each of these special demands, I find with a kind of terror that what is demanded is nothing less than the simultaneous and systematic abolition of all laws and all customs obtaining in the country; I see immediately that it is going to be a question of one of the most extensive and dangerous revolutions the world has ever seen.'

The French were walking into revolution backwards, ' . . . for the complete absence of all political liberty rendered the world of affairs not merely unfamiliar but actually invisible.' The interest of this situation for a student of nationalism is that it is typical of fully developed nationalist politics, typical indeed of what has come to be called an 'ideological style of politics'. The roots of this style no doubt go back to the religious dissensions of the sixteenth century.

Something rather similar is found in the Anabaptists (whose behaviour at Münster in 1534–5 strikingly resembles that of the Jacobins of the 1790s) and in the English Puritans, who also looked forward to a new reign of righteousness. In all these cases, we find a class of people who have not participated in the day-to-day running of a government believing that they could create a new era if only they controlled the levers of political power. Such hopes arise from an intense belief in a doctrine.

One reason for this intense belief may again be culled from de Tocqueville: 'One can say generally that in the eighteenth century Christianity had lost a great part of its power over the entire continent of Europe.' Irreligion had become a 'dominant and widespread passion'. Here again, one's expectations are overturned. For it might seem that a growth of religious infidelity, following centuries of religious fanaticism and war, would lead increasingly to toleration. This is certainly what the *philosophes* themselves seem to have believed. What in fact happened was the rapid growth of political intolerance, reproducing both in its fanaticism and in the structure of its doctrines just those theologies which had seemed to be weakening. The obvious—perhaps too obvious—inference is that religious passions had been transferred to politics; and that political ideologies had come to constitute new religions.

We must not take this analogy too far. Nationalism and liberalism are *not* religions, though some men may cling to them as if they were. We may further elucidate the connection between philosophy and fanaticism if we look to a clue which has often struck those who have studied the eighteenth century. The clue is this: philosophers of this period became greatly preoccupied with education. They wrote books about it, and they hoped that education would solve the political evils of the world. There is a perfectly general argument, which in one version was persuasively advanced by Burke in his *Reflections on the Revolution in France*, which suggests that the man who mistakes politics for education is likely to become a fanatic.

The argument distinguishes between politics and philosophy. Philosophy is concerned with truth. Is the good definable? Does the earth move in an elliptical path round the sun? Can values be derived validly from factual propositions? Many such questions are no doubt difficult, but if they are properly formulated, then in principle there is a right and a wrong answer. Contrast politics. It is about whether the state should increase expenditure on defence or spend more on the social services. Should the franchise be extended to all adults? Ought strikes to be permitted in wartime? No doubt there are factual issues involved in discussing these questions, but they can never be reduced to issues of truth. Politics is a matter of balancing conflicting interests, demands and guesses. Compromise is the usual result of negotiation; in philosophy it is generally a sign of confusion. Philosophers *may* educate each other (and their pupils) because they are co-operating in the pursuit of a single type of goal—true beliefs. Politicians must negotiate with each other in pursuit of conflicting goals. (They may not, of course, and then they will come to blows.)

If this is true, then the man who confuses politics with philosophy will begin to imagine that he can enlighten those he negotiates with. And if they refuse to be 'enlightened', then he is likely to turn nasty. One of the perennial dangers of education is that it may turn into a battle of wills between the educator and his pupil. The situation is even worse if (like the eighteenth-century *philosophe*) our educator believes he is dealing in rational truths, for a rational truth is by definition accessible to the understanding of any sane man. Our educator-politician, in his frustration, is likely to demand: What is this fellow doing who opposes what I know to be truth? And both the tone and the content of his likely answer are typified in the Encyclopaedia's entry on prostitution: 'The meaning of these words *prostitute* and *prostitution* has been stretched to cover those critics of whom there are today so many . . . writers of whom one says that they *prostitute* their pens for money, for favour, for lying, envy and vices unworthy of a well-bred man. Whilst literature was abandoned to these pests, philosophy on the other hand was defamed by a troupe of petty crooks, lacking in knowledge, wit and morality, who for their part *prostituted* themselves to men who were not displeased to see disparaged in the eyes of the nation those who might enlighten it on their mischief and triviality.' Fanaticism does not cease to be fanaticism because it affirms the noblest aspirations; even tolerance may be fanatically espoused.

The *philosophes* were tempted to brush aside discussions of conflicting interest and reduce all questions to matters of abstract truth. This made them prone to fanaticism. But the process might just as easily work in reverse: just as the *philosophes* 'reduced' interests to a matter of truth, so others might attempt to 'reduce' truth to a matter of interests.

We then find a violent assertion of the value of the particular—*my* nation, *my* language, *my* customs—against a universalist preoccupation with reason and humanity. It only makes sense as a reaction to an already prevailing universalistic system. French cosmopolitanism was the system against which the early nationalists reacted. We may understand what happened by comparing it to the industrial revolution. The British were pioneers of modern industry. They early developed inventions and factories which could produce industrial goods more cheaply and efficiently than anyone else. Understandably enough—so later nationalists argued—they developed an economic theory which supported free trade, for under conditions of free trade, all goods are produced where they can be made most efficiently. Free trade is a plausible policy for just so long as everyone believes in the overall advantages of one economic system. But sooner rather than later, non-industrial countries will seek to establish secondary industries of their own, and then they will break up the system by building protective tariffs round their infant industries. This is what the Americans and the Germans did as they became caught up in industrial growth. Similarly, the *philosophes* may be seen as the pioneers of an intellectual revolution. They believed in a free trade in ideas, for they were the most efficient processors of ideas. But their domination of the cultural world was bound in time to provoke a defensive reaction from the intellectual classes arising in other parts of Europe. Even Goethe, who throughout his life rejected the role of national symbol and remained true to the Enlightenment, complained that the French (like mathematicians) converted everything into the French language, and thereby changed its content. The materials for this intellectual protectionism were being put together in the eighteenth century by Herder; but the nationalist significance of what he did can only be understood as a reaction to the cultural hegemony of France.

The Patriotism of Jean-Jacques Rousseau

We saw in the last chapter that nationalist ideology is prone to see all past history in its own terms. It does this by claiming patriotism as its own. We also saw that patriotism is quite different from nationalism. It is true, however, that if we wish to trace the evolution of nationalist ideas, we must look to what was happening to patriotism in the period before a fully fledged nationalism can be said to exist.

A patriot is a man who looks at his own country, likes it, and is ready to make sacrifices for it. Jean-Jacques Rousseau looked at his part of the world and experienced little else but loathing. A native of Geneva, he spent most of his life in France or Switzerland. Commonly regarded as a ridiculous figure by the *philosophes*, he suffered considerable ill-treatment at their hands. He seems to have magnified this ill-treatment by indulging in delusions of persecution. He brought to the task of denouncing current civilisation not only a sparkling prose style but also a moral fervour not commonly found in the flippancies of his fellow-intellectuals. To denounce the follies of one's time is older than the prophet Jeremiah; and Christian civilisation has seldom lacked men who thought that the times had never been so bad before. But Rousseau, at one bound, leapt into a specifically modern type of denunciation. 'It is clear', he wrote, 'that we must also place to the credit of the property system, and consequently society, assassinations, poisonings, highway robberies, and even the punishments inflicted for these crimes—punishments necessary to prevent greater evils, which yet for the murder of one man, cost the life of two or more, thus doubling the waste of humanity.'[4] He raged over the commercial corruption that results from greed, lamented the miseries of the arranged marriage, discoursed on the enfeeblement of populations given over to luxury and on the tribes of beggars who infested cities. When he wrote that 'it is plainly contrary to the law of nature, however defined, that children should command old men, fools wise men, and that the privileged few should gorge themselves with superfluities, while the starving multitude are in want of the bare necessities of life', he plucked a chord of modern feeling which has not ceased vibrating from his day to ours.

Like later socialists, it is the wasteful system of commerce which is the central target of his hatred. He hates rich merchants, intellectuals writing to please the crowd, theatrical spectacles, enterprising seducers, and men whose behaviour seems entirely determined by private desire and insincere conventions. In a word, he hates individualism. When he comes to philosophise, he therefore rejects the dominant social contract theory which had for the preceding century been the prevailing rationalisation of that mode of behaviour. Rousseau's version of social contract is not an expedient by which men pursue more efficiently the same private interests which moved them in a state of nature; it is a process of moralisation by which human beings develop moral capacities forgotten or suppressed under the prevailing system of society. The successful arrival of citizens at this admirable condition is indicated by the presence of the general will—the decision willed by a community of citizens who put the public good before all else. The general will is always right, and it is always what the people of a 'legitimate society' will decide. It is a puzzling idea, arising out of a complex set of preoccupations. Our concern is not with what the general will might actually be, but with the vulgarisations of the idea which became current after Rousseau's death.

The common way of summing up Rousseau's place in the history of thought is to say that he was the prophet of a growing sense of community. The sense of community seems to have been a yearning for something long lost—a yearning for those traditional certainties which were being undermined by the growth of commerce. The state in France had for more than a century been drawing power from the provinces. France appeared to many Frenchmen an irrational conglomerate of private interests held together by nothing more than the weight of a centralising monarchy. It taxed, and it consumed the taxes, but it appeared to give little in return. It was remote and arbitrary. Frenchmen seem to have been torn between a growing and genuine sense of attachment to 'France' and a miserable dislike of the class hatreds which they attributed to surviving feudal inequalities. Rousseau supplied much the profoundest expression of their longing that the French state might turn into a community.

He was, as we have said, a patriot without a *patrie*. What was admirable did not exist, and what existed was far from admirable.

Rousseau's solution was to become a patriot of the ancient world. 'He who reads ancient history finds himself transported into another world and among other beings.'[5] The ancients look larger than life; yet they were real. Why are we so different? Rousseau attributed modern inferiority to 'our low philosophy, and petty passions, concentrated with egoism in every heart by inept institutions which lack the inspiration of a genius'. Lycurgus is praised as a legislator who kept *la patrie* before the eyes of Spartans, in the laws, in games, in festivals, in all human life. Contrast this with the indistinguishability of modern men. 'There are today no longer Frenchmen, Germans, Spaniards, even Englishmen', he wrote, 'there are only Europeans. . . . Provided they find money to steal and women to corrupt, they are everywhere at home.'

These reflections, straight from the heart, were inspired by the vision of Poland as a country ripe for remoulding by a philosophic legislator. Poland for a brief moment was for Rousseau what Syracuse was for Plato. Yet he made Poland the object of a specifically modern kind of hope—that out of a terrible crisis the Polish nation would experience a rebirth. The beginning of a new epoch, he thought, depended upon correct principles of education. 'It is the test of education to give to each human being a national form, and so direct his opinions and tastes, that he should be a patriot by inclination, by passion, by necessity. On first opening his eyes, a child must see his country, and until he dies, must see nothing else.'[6] There are many such passages scattered through Rousseau. They reveal his habit of using *nation* and *patrie* interchangeably—though as the emotion of a passion rises, Rousseau will usually discard *nation* for *patrie*. Further, this is not merely a matter of producing men whose unselfish devotion to the public good is unshakeable: Rousseau wants the Poles to have a 'national physiognomy which will distinguish them from all other people'. 'At twenty', Rousseau wrote, 'a Pole must not be just another man; he must be a Pole.' National education ought therefore to move in stages. A child learning to read must be saturated in his country's traditions. At 10 he must know its products, at 12 its provinces, roads and towns, at 15 its history and at 16 its laws. His heart and mind must be filled with the illustrious men and noble acts of its legend. Even education, however, has its danger, for teachers may turn into a profession with a vested interest. The true lawgiver, or in modern terms, social engineer, must ensure that the role of citizen dominates all others. Even the metaphor of engineering is inadequate: 'soul-moulding' is really what Rousseau is up to, and even law is an inadequate instrument. 'Simplicity of custom and dress is less the fruit of Law than of education.' And again: 'Whoever essays to institute a people must know how to dominate the opinions, and thereby the passions, of men.'

In order to grasp the fatuity of this dream, we need only remember that Poland in the later Middle Ages was one of the most populous and cultivated of European states. It had, of course, fallen on evil days, but it was a long way from being the blank sheet which alone would make Rousseau's suggestions practicable. On the other hand, we must beware of seeing in this kind of writing the ancestor of the modern totalitarian state. It should be obvious that Rousseau, far from being the harbinger of the future, was in fact dominated by an overpowering nostalgia for the past.

Rousseau used the word 'nation' but is far from being a nationalist. He expressed what seems to have been becoming a typical desire to belong to a community which should not be criss-crossed by local and class hatreds. Above all, he has the passion to *make* a community which he *will* love, like a woman marrying a drunkard in order to reform him. Such an aspiration is very likely to produce only frustration, especially in a modern world wherein there are too many moulders and not enough characters suitable for moulding.

Political writing falls on the attention not of simple students waiting to be instructed, but of men and women dominated by special preoccupations of their own. Now the word *nation* had already in France a very special history of its own. For many articulate Frenchmen, *nation* was almost a technical term in a long-standing debate on the question: Who were the French? To this we must next turn.

Who Were the French?

What is called the history of France is for hundreds of years the history of two distinct things. One is the history of centralising dynasties like the Capetians, the Valois and the Bourbons. These were successions of kings based on the Ile de France who steadily accumulated power over neighbouring feudal powers and, remembering Gaul and the empire of Charlemagne, claimed ascendancy in many parts of what we now call France. The other history is the history of the peoples and rulers inhabiting the territory we *now* call France. But that territory has included such languages as the Basque, the Breton and the Provençale. There have been periods when Southern France looked across the Pyrenees rather than north to Paris. The political independence of the Midi was crushed by the Albigensian crusade. Later southern moves to opt out of France were defeated after the religious wars between Catholic and Huguenot. There have also been times when the kings of England—Norman and Plantagenet—ruled more of France than did its own kings. It was but an incident of this complicated history when under Louis XIV some Frenchmen thought that the 'natural' boundaries of France were the Pyrenees, the Alps and the Rhine. This argument, beginning in diplomatic statecraft, came later to be a genuine component of French nationalism.

The politics of France were for a long time argued out in terms of the question: Who were the French? According to convenience, the French, or a relevant part of them, might be traced back to Gallic, Frankish or even Roman elements. A great stimulus was given to French historical writing by the fact that large contemporary issues depended upon what the 'historian' might be able to demonstrate about the relations between Clovis, his Frankish followers, and the Gallic population he found in the country. In the sixteenth century, this argument was used for and against absolute centralisation of government. Early in the seventeenth century, Henry IV and his minister Sully repaired many of the ravages of the wars of religion by extending the system of *Intendants*, royal officials established throughout the provinces, men whose power depended on royal appointment, and who were periodically moved around to prevent their loyalties being absorbed by the locality in which they worked. This system fell to pieces on the assassination of Henry in 1610. The *parlement*, the nobles and the localities rallied to destroy a system which threatened them. Under Louis XIII, Richelieu revived and

continued the system of centralisation, weakening the power of the
nobility, and destroying the political potential of the Huguenots.
Again, the system foundered after Richelieu's death, but once
Louis XIV was firmly established, France became decisively cen-
tralised. This struggle was not, however, simply one between a
dominating centre and a periphery; it was also between absolutism
and feudalism, and although royal absolutism established itself
beyond any serious threat, the aristocracy retained not merely their
feudal privileges (such as taxation exemptions) but also their sense of
constituting a separate and superior caste within the French state.

The main criticism of Louis XIV's absolutism came in the seventeenth century from aristocratic writers like Fenelon, Saint-Simon
and Boulainvilliers. What they resented was the use by the king of
bourgeois ministers whom he could make or break at will. They
advocated a limited monarchy which they supposed had been the
system prevailing in the days of Charlemagne. The primary limitation
was that the king should share his power with the nobility. They
admitted, indeed, that the nobility had become scattered and
infiltrated by non-noble elements. The nobility should therefore be
reformed. Fenelon argued that the king should regenerate this class
by the device of a strict registration and control of titles. Misalliances
and illegitimacy should be forbidden, and the purified nobility should
have a monopoly of military and political functions.

Boulainvilliers, early in the eighteenth century, argued that the
French nobility was descended from the Franks who, by their conquest of Gaul, had acquired certain rights over the territory and
certain privileges over the conquered Gauls, which were the origin
and the legitimate source of the nobles' prerogatives throughout
French history.[7] The French 'nation', in the more technical sense,
was a constitution in which the king, the nobles and the Third Estate
played their traditional roles in the determination of government.
The French, in a less technical sense, consisted of two 'nations', the
Franks and the Gallo-Romans. The Franks composed the First and
Second Estates (for Boulainvilliers argued that the clergy had
traditionally consisted of the nobility). The Third Estate descended
from the conquered Gauls. It will be obvious that Rousseau's
arguments (especially in the first chapters of the *Social Contract*) that

Might is no legitimate source of Right, constitute an implicit criticism of this position.

In 1608, Pierre Cayet had written in criticism of Francis Hotman: ' . . . In short he scrimmaged with old histories, rightly or wrongly, according to his passions.' These passions varied from time to time according to the political issue which was dominant. But one passion which grew in intensity in the centuries before 1789 was the social resentment of the bourgeoisie against the nobility. When the Estates General met for the last time before the Revolution, in 1614, they proved intractable and had the doors shut in their faces. 'Are we today', they demanded plaintively, 'any different from what we were yesterday before the king, or has one night changed our status and authority?' But they were powerless to act. The aristocracy in 1614 refused to 'have the sons of cobblers and shoemakers call them brothers'. They did not consider themselves related 'to the vulgar in the closest of society, which is fraternity'. It was precisely that fraternity which became the rallying cry of the revolutionaries, and which signalises the nationalist element of the French Revolution.

In the rationalist atmosphere of the eighteenth century, there were many who refused to take this historical argument seriously. Voltaire, for example, wrote that Clovis was but 'the leader of possibly 20,000 ill-dressed and ill-armed barbarians, who conquered eight or ten million Gauls held in servitude by three or four Roman legions'. He mocked the entire argument: 'I have but lately read a book beginning: "The Franks, from whom we are descended. . . ." Halloo, my friend, who told you that you were descended in a straight line from a Frank?' His mockery weakened, but it did not entirely kill the habit of deriving English liberties or French valour from the supposed moral qualities of barbarian tribes in the forests of Germany—tribes of whom Voltaire remarked that 'like all the other barbarians of the North, [they were] ferocious beasts who sought food, lodging, and a few rags against the snow'.[8]

Voltaire did, however, feel powerfully the hatred of aristocratic privilege which animated so many of his contemporaries. His contemporary Mably edged the historical argument towards a radical conclusion. He attacked the 'insolence and brutality' the French had brought with them from Germany, and the Roman corruptions which led to the transformation of French society into the fiefs, *corvées*, tolls and dues of the feudal system. The interest of these arguments for us is that a social struggle has been conceptualised as a struggle between two 'nations' inhabiting the same territory. For noble and bourgeois alike, France was conceived after the manner of a conquered and occupied territory. In the writings of the Abbé Sieyès, we may see the use the Revolution made of this set of ideas.

Sieyès and the French Revolution

In the work of the Abbé Sieyès, we find a number of these streams of thought converging. Sieyès for a very brief period after 1789 imposed himself upon his contemporaries as the spokesman of the new era, and especially—as the Swiss lawyer Dumont put it—the 'oracle of the Third Estate'. We have already seen that the Third Estate of 1614, finding itself dismissed, had merely protested. In 1789, when the same thing happened, Sieyès expressed a new spirit: 'We are today everything we were yesterday. Let us deliberate!' This confident spirit was partly no doubt produced by the new wealth and power of the French bourgeoisie; but it also bespoke the intellectual conviction of two generations of Enlightenment. Everything was to be put on a rational basis. 'Politics', Sieyès told Dumont, 'is a science I believe I have mastered.'

Sieyès produced a kind of knockabout metaphysics, moving from historical to rational arguments as served his purpose. That purpose, for all the long passages of pure abstraction, was to influence his fellow politicians. They were all intellectuals; he appealed to them in intellectual terms. 'I want', he began his first pamphlet, the *Essay on Privileges*, 'to examine privileges in their origin, nature and effects.'[9] The origin purported to be the Frankish conquest. Sieyès was happy to accept the argument of Boulainvilliers, but he has new conclusions to draw from it. The nobility are a foreign element in France, descended from a race of conquerors. Why then ought not the French to repatriate them to the Franconian forests whence they came? They constitute a nation within the nation, and the social system they embody is a standing humiliation for the French people. The French—that is, the Gauls—remain in servitude so long as this feudal domination continues. What then is the Third Estate? It is everything. It is not merely one of the three Estates of France, but the nation itself, and that which does not belong to it, that which is alienated by privilege, is no part of France.

What is dynamic in Sieyès—and what seems to have harmonised with the mood of his audience—was the astonishing mixture of a rational apparatus with the most ungovernable hatred. Sieyès was an early exponent of philosophical violence. ' . . . the blood boils', he wrote, 'at the mere thought that it is possible to give *legal recognition*, at the close of the eighteenth century, to the abominable fruits of abominable feudalism.' Or again: 'When the philosopher is driving a road, he is concerned with errors; to make progress he must destroy them without pity.' This is a revealing slip, for there is clearly no question of pitying errors, only of being tolerant of the people who cling to them. Sieyès and his generation were screwing themselves up to that ruthlessness which brought the guillotine into the business of destroying errors. *Couic!* There goes another fallacy! One of the commonest metaphors Sieyès used to describe the privileged class was that of 'some horrible disease eating the living flesh on the body of some unfortunate man'. It 'is a plague for the nation which suffers it.'

A privilege is, then, a disease which Dr Sieyès would cure. 'By privileged, I mean any man who stands outside common rights, either because he claims freedom *in every respect* from subjection to the common laws, or because he claims exclusive rights.'[10] Privileges are desired by men because of the 'intoxicating charm' of superiority, but they are incompatible with liberty and self-respect. The privileged constitute a 'nation chosen within the nation' and their first thoughts are for the interest of that narrow caste, not for the nation itself. Indeed, the privileged come to think of themselves as a different species of beings from ordinary men. Privilege is incompatible with the recognition of one's common humanity. Sieyès makes the concept of 'privilege' a master-idea by which he organises the multiplicity of social grievances felt by Frenchmen in 1788. In these two pamphlets we feel the stinging recoil of hurt pride, and a thousand never-forgotten humiliations mobilise a keen intelligence into a comprehensive review of the social situation of the nobility. The privileged are cut off from the French nation by the racial heritage they claim, by the idleness they cultivate, even indeed (and here Sieyès touches on one of the grand preoccupations of nationalism) by the very language they speak. 'I shall not try to express', he wrote, 'all the nuances, all the finesse of the habitual language of the privileged. We should need for this language a special dictionary which would be new in more than one way; for, instead of containing the proper or metaphorical sense of the words, it would need, on the contrary, to detach from words their true meaning, leaving nothing but emptiness from a rational point of view—but admirably profound meanings for the privileged.'[11] He proceeded to poke fun at elliptical aristocratic use of words like *naissance* (for only the rich have birth), *grace*, *qualité*, *origine*, *hommes d'hier*, etc. It is clear that the nation will speak but one language, even down to the *nuances*.

The concept of the nation is used by Sieyès as a battering-ram against this entrenched array of privilege. What is the nation? It is 'a body of associates living under *common* laws and represented by the same legislative assembly'.[12] Fundamentally, this nation consists of the Third Estate; it is open, however, to all Frenchmen, and Sieyès wrote that the nation 'will remember with gratitude the patriotic writers of the first two orders who were the first to abjure archaic errors and preferred the principles of universal justice to the murderous conspiracies of corporate interest against the interest of the nation.' All that is good and public-spirited is allocated to the concept 'nation', all that is evil and selfish fits in with the idea 'privilege'. The idea of the nation is then developed in abstract terms: 'The nation is prior to everything. It is the source of everything. Its will is always legal; indeed it is the law itself. Prior to and above the nation, there is only *natural* law. . . . Every attribute of the nation springs from the simple fact that it exists.'[13] This last phrase is a parody of the ontological argument for the existence of God; when Sieyès moves into this gear, he usually produces a string of metaphysician's clichés. Most of it is a refraction of Rousseau, but it lacks Rousseau's painful awareness of complexities and comes tripping off the pen.

Like Rousseau, Sieyès is thinking primarily in terms of the harmonious community. The passion for national unity seems to have been felt at all social levels. Professor Carleton Hayes quotes from a conscript's letter: 'It is to the nation . . . to which everything belongs.'[14] This is hardly a philosophical idea, and the people who might have yielded assent to that proposition were no doubt many of them confused and inconsistent. But this view summarises the behaviour of thousands of young Frenchmen who in those few years voluntarily gave up their comfort and their private ambitions in order to march off to repel the allied armies who, supporting the king's cause, were invading French soil. An excellent eye-witness account of how it felt is found in Stendhal's *Vie de Napoléon*, describing the atmosphere of 1794:

In our eyes, the inhabitants of the rest of Europe who fought to keep their chains were pitiable imbeciles, or rascals in the pay of the despots who attacked us. *Pitt* and *Coburg*, whose names are still heard repeated in the old echo of the Revolution, seemed to us the leaders of those scoundrels and the personification of everything that was treacherous and stupid in the world. Everything was then dominated by a deep feeling of which I can no longer see any trace. If he is less than 50, let the reader imagine to himself, according to the books, that in 1794 we had no sort of religion at all; our deep and inner feelings were compounded in this one idea: *being useful to our country.*

Everything else—clothing, food, promotion—were in our eyes only miserable and ephemeral details. As there was no society, being *socially successful*, so important an element in the character of our nation, did not exist for us.

In the street, our eyes would fill with tears on coming across a wall inscription in honour of the young drummer boy Barra (who got himself killed at 13 years of age rather than stop beating his drum, in order to prevent a surprise attack). For us who knew no other social world, there were festivals, numerous and touching ceremonies, which came along to nourish the sentiment which dominated everything in our hearts.

It was our only religion. When Napoleon appeared to put an end to the continual blunders to which the dreary government of the Directory exposed us, we saw in him only the *military utility* of dictatorship. He gave us victories, but we judged all his actions by the rules of the religion which, from our first childhood, made our hearts beat faster. We saw nothing admirable in it but *utility to our country*.[15]

These feelings were to become part of the legend of the French Revolution. They were fitted into the story of an oppressed people, driven beyond endurance, who rose up and took the control of society into their own hands, demonstrating in the process how irresistible was the might of a people aroused. The story turns into tragedy as the heroes jockey for position, get caught up in the difficult judgments of the national situation, and finally succumb to mediocrity with the fall of Robespierre in Thermidor 1794. This story has become the beacon of all subsequent radical movements, even of those who hated everything the Revolution thought it stood for. But above all, in later French nationalist thought, the Revolution stood for the most persistent kind of dream in the literature of nationalism—the dream of harmony. Here is the historian Michelet writing more than a generation later: 'France was born and started into life at the sound of the cannon of the Bastille. . . . I do not believe that the heart of man was at any period more teeming with a vast and comprehensive affection, or that the distinctions of classes, fortunes and parties, were ever so much forgotten. In the villages, especially, there are no longer either rich or poor, nobles or plebeians; there is but one general table, and provisions are in common; social dissensions and quarrels have disappeared; enemies become reconciled; and opposite sects, believers and philosophers, Protestants and Catholics fraternize together. . . .'[16] This ignores the mass executions which took place all over France, the civil war in the Vendée, the festering enmities among politicians which culminated in Thermidor, and the hysteria with which individuals immolated themselves on the altar of the *patrie*. Yet the fact that this rustic echo of Rousseau was not entirely invention may be attested from the memoirs of many who lived through the experience.

It might seem that we have here reached a fully developed nationalism. Professor Carleton Hayes talks of 'Jacobin nationalism' as embodied in the careers of such men as Bertrand Barère and

Lazare Carnot. He contrasts this democratic nationalism with the aristocratic nationalism of Bolingbroke and the cultural nationalism of Herder, and thinks that it is characterised by four features: it was intolerant of internal dissent, it relied upon force and militarism, it was fanatically religious, and marked by a missionary zeal.[17] A further sign of nationalism might be detected in Sieyès's attitude to the English Constitution: 'I do not deny that the English Constitution is an astonishing work for its time. Nevertheless, although people are always ready to sneer at a Frenchman who does not prostrate himself before it, I am bold enough to say that I do not find in it the simplicity of good order, but rather a framework of precautions against disorder.'

But the clue to the meaning of Sieyès's dislike of the English Constitution is given in a later passage: 'After all, why do we think so much of this exotic Constitution? Apparently, because it comes close to the principles of the good society. But if ideal models of the beautiful and the good exist to guide us, and if, moreover, we are unable to say that the ideal model of society is less well known to us now than it was to the English in 1688, how then can we disregard the true good and be satisfied with imitating its copy?'[18]

This is Rationalism, not Nationalism. It looks to an ideal model which is valid for all mankind: that is, Sieyès was not thinking of the uniqueness of France, and of a constitution which should be especially appropriate to her peculiar genius; he was still thinking of humanity. And in this he was typical of the Revolutionary period. He did of course make frequent use of the *word* 'nation' and he is part of the history of nationalism precisely because he helped to give it currency. He needed the word 'nation' partly because of its place in the long historical argument we considered in the last section; and partly because he did not wish to use the word *people*. He was a radical, but he was not a democrat: 'It is unquestionable that tramps and beggars cannot be charged with the political confidence of nations. Would a servant or any person under the domination of a master, or a non-naturalised foreigner, be permitted to appear among the representatives of the nation?'[19] The nation in this context is the community conceived as politically active; it is the moral substance of which the state is merely the shadow. It carries many of the undertones of *patrie* without dragging in its train the unwantedly radical possibilities inherent in *people*.

The French Revolution began as an internal social struggle rationalised as a conflict between the principle of privilege and the principle of national equality. As it developed, it became also a struggle between France and the other countries of Europe—a national struggle perhaps. But this revolutionary war was never adequately rationalised as a national struggle. It was always seen as a war of liberation—a social struggle spilling across the out-dated dynastic borders of Europe. It always retained a strong element of universality. Nationalism is the reaction of the particular to the universal; and it is just because the French Revolution was universalist that nationalism was an adequate response to it.

3

Nationalism and German Unity

There is an abyss between the men of brilliant and facile
conceptions and men of brutal deeds and active bestiality
which no intellectual explanation is able to bridge.

Hannah Arendt[1]

Political Ideas in the Nineteenth Century

The nineteenth century brought a distinct change in the intellectual
atmosphere of Europe. This is partly to be accounted for by social
changes, and partly by the domination of certain highly general ideas
which deeply affected nationalists everywhere.

Who were the nationalists? By definition, they were intellectuals.
This class of people increased in numbers throughout the century. In
Napoleonic Germany, nationalist enthusiasm was limited to the
intellectual middle classes who were a tiny part of the population. In
Prussia in 1805 there were about 1,500 university students in all.[2] But
literacy and education expanded at a faster rate even than population,
and brought with it an expansion in books, newspapers and
pamphlets. It led, also, to the beginnings of a written literature in
many languages and dialects—in Czech, Magyar, Rumanian, Croat,
etc. Journalists, civil servants and, in time, trade-union and party
officials all came to swell the numbers of the intellectual classes.
Many of them were self-educated craftsmen or skilled workers whose
enthusiasm for literacy and passion for understanding overcame the
handicap of having had no formal training.

Many of these men were eager consumers of political ideas, because
the hopes which many in earlier centuries would have invested in
religious salvation had now come to be transferred to politics. They

were the spiritual descendants of the heretics and puritans of earlier centuries. They passed their lives reading the journals of their persuasion, attending party meetings, passing resolutions, and eagerly following the course of politics all over Europe. It seemed to have become the duty of European man to have political opinions, and the source of this duty was a belief in the benefits of democracy.

Most of them had a millennial view of history. 'And today', wrote Mazzini, 'the times *are* ripe.'[3] The question in dispute was what exactly the times were ripe *for*. Richard Wagner believed that contemporary artists had necessarily to be political, and that pure poetry would only be possible after the revolution.[4] Friedrich Jahn, who belonged to the first generation of German nationalists wrote: 'In the whole history of a people, its most sacred moment arrives when it awakens from its torpor, becomes for the first time conscious of itself, thinks of its sacred rights and of the eternal duty of preserving them.'[5] And Marx believed that a new world was being born. All these feelings were concentrated on the concept of 'revolution', which had ceased to be something which happened to the stars, and had come to convey the climax of a political struggle. Every politically conscious man had, as a result of the French Revolution, a picture of revolutions in his head—the turbulent crowds, ripping up cobblestones, beating back the assaults of soldiers in colourful uniforms.

The concept of revolution was closely associated with an admiration for struggle. It was engagement in struggle which was thought to mobilise the heroic virtues in men. Hegel's dialectical philosophy rationalised the operations of struggle in history and in logic, and later in the century Darwinism was thought to demonstrate that humanity itself had emerged from the struggle between organic life and its environment. In ethics, the central concept of this romantic doctrine was Duty, a term which demands capitals by virtue of the reverence in which it was held. The nineteenth century could, in terms of its serious concern with Duty, characterise itself as morally wholesome by contrast with the Enlightenment's emphasis on rights. Whereas their predecessors had thought of pleasure as the key principle of ethics, the men of the nineteenth century detected all manner of purifying effects in the suffering which necessarily accompanied a struggle.

This is, of course, something of a caricature. The legacy of the eighteenth century could not be so easily thrown off, and those who justified their behaviour in terms of duty were inevitably criticised in terms of duty's shadow: hypocrisy. Radicals and socialists carried on the traditions of the Enlightenment, and were commonly hostile to the milieu which produced nationalism. The spirit of the age, between one generation and another, produced profound differences. Jeremy Bentham is temperamentally a very different figure from John Stuart Mill, and even further from imperialist radicals such as Dilke and Joseph Chamberlain later in the century.

Men who choose to live lives of struggle must in politics fight against oppression and exploitation. And in the nineteenth century they had the choice of struggling against foreign oppression or class oppression. Those who fought foreign oppression (real or imaginary) developed the theory of the nation and sought to unify all members of the nation into an organic whole, thinking and feeling as one. In Mazzini's generation, they could imagine that once every people had attained its own nation-state, then peace would prevail in the world. But from about the middle of the century, it was becoming perfectly clear that national unity involved international disunity, and in some cases a positive admiration of wars as the supreme school of the heroic national virtues. Those, on the other hand, who chose to wage the class struggle tended to develop international connections and to attack nationalism as a middle-class doctrine designed to distract the workers from social issues. Socialists and radicals consequently inherited the rationalist universalism of the Enlightenment. But both nationalists and socialists insisted that theirs was the essential struggle.

Both groups of political intellectuals, however, had developed a historical awareness seldom found in the eighteenth century. A good illustration of this type of awareness is a famous passage in Burke's *Reflections on the Revolution in France*. 'Society is indeed a contract,' Burke wrote, ' . . . It is a partnership in all science; a partnership in all art; a partnership in every virtue, and in all perfection. As the ends of such a partnership cannot be obtained in many generations, it becomes a partnership not only between those who are living, but between those who are living, those who are dead, and those who are to be born. Each contract of each particular state is but a clause in the great primaeval contract of eternal society, linking the lower with the higher natures, connecting the visible and invisible world, according to a fixed compact sanctioned by the inviolable oath which holds all physical and all moral natures, each in their appointed place.' Here Burke has taken the classical doctrine of the social contract and transposed it into an entirely new key, rather like the tune of a pop song used as a theme for symphonic variations. The social contract was a limited doctrine, but Burke extended it into 'every virtue' and 'all perfection'. In its original form, the contract was part of a rationalised history of mankind in which human beings met together and for practical reasons constructed themselves a state. Burke's version, for all its metaphysics, directs our attention to the actual details of the history of our institutions as the only valid way of explaining what they are. And in Burke's version, we may detect a nostalgia for an ordered and hierarchical society ('each in his appointed place')—a nostalgia such as might be expected to afflict men who are suffering the disruption of the industrial revolution. Burke was greatly admired by the German romantic thinkers who, as part of their rejection of French rationalism, constructed a romantic picture of the Middle Ages.

This passage further illustrates the hunger for profundity which led men to condemn the Enlightenment as shallow and superficial. Politics is seen as part of a cosmic scheme, in which the sense of an invisible world supplies a meaning for the procession of events in the everyday world of politics. One common result of this new sensibility was an addiction to theosophy. Joseph de Maistre, for example, believed in a higher and wiser race of men who lived before the Deluge; and Mazzini thought that this life of ours is only an episode in the life of the soul, an intermediate step in the ladder that leads to God.[6] Theosophy is in many ways a natural complement to nationalism, since both consist of vague sets of ideas which can be combined and recombined according to the passions of the moment. They can be fitted together to make up a philosophy of history which explains to believers what is their situation in the present struggle.

It must be added that the passage from Burke is also the portent of a decline of intellectual clarity which is always likely to accompany a hunger for profundity. Burke begins with a clear idea, and turns rhetorical; his words become less a statement of a thought than a means of expressing an emotion he feels. There is indeed here a complicated idea which he is attempting to convey; but his manner of doing so is likely to corrupt lesser men.

Herder and National Individuality

Johann Gottfried von Herder, who died in 1803, was a slightly younger contemporary of Edmund Burke. He was not quite a philosopher, nor a literary critic, nor a creative writer; on the other hand, he was more than a *belles-lettriste*. J. L. Talmon writes of him as a man of 'epoch-making intimations and premonitions'.[7] Nietzsche said he was neither creator nor critic, but 'an unquiet guest' at the banquet of German culture. Rather in the manner of Rousseau, his personality was an equilibrium of conflicting passions. He seems to have been a complex neurotic who admired simple, rooted people. Seldom feeling at home anywhere, he envied those who 'belonged'. He is often remembered for his failures—for the ambition to become a surgeon which ended when he fainted at his first dissection, and for his astonishment on arriving at Nantes and discovering that he could not understand a word of French. But he wrote a lot, and supplied nationalism with its theory of the nation.

For us, whose concern is simply with Herder's contribution to nationalism, his central idea is that of the *Volk*. The *Volk* is not simply the people of a country, but a metaphysical entity defined relationally as *that which* produces a particular language, art, culture, set of great men, religion and collection of customs. All of these things are taken, not as the products of individual men but as *manifestations* of the spirit of the people, or *Volksgeist*. *Hamlet* was written (one assumes) by Shakespeare; but the significance of Shakespeare to a nationalist thinker is that he is an expression of what is highest in the English *Volk*. We have moved therefore from the precise statement 'Shakespeare wrote *Hamlet*' to the more high-sounding but also much vaguer assertion 'the English *Volk* created *Hamlet*'.

Stated in this bald manner, the doctrine looks odd. Both Herder and those who followed him much preferred to discuss communal products as the best illustrations of the activity of the *Volksgeist*—particularly language, myths and legends, folksongs and folktales. The very anonymity of such productions was a virtue in that it appeared to guarantee that they were spontaneous and free from the egoism of the man who signs his work. One of the consequences of Herder's writings was to set off a prodigious amount of folkloristic and philological research which everywhere accompanied the growth of European nationalism.[8]

Logically, the novelty of these views lay in what was taken as fundamental. The *philosophes* had generally operated with the idea of a human nature which was assumed to be fundamentally invariable. Differences in people's customs from one area to another were to be explained as the result of accident and local circumstance. The concept of human nature was elaborated in the psychological terms of reason and passion. Moral and political ideas were derived from this assumed human nature, and they were therefore in principle universally relevant. But Herder regarded the common human nature shared by all men as a trivial abstraction. Men are always found in divided groups which have evolved a language and culture in response to their environment and which express their own national character. In the succession of generations, a people elaborates and develops that culture; and each individual man is what he is because one or another culture has stamped itself upon him.

The concept of the *Volk* is, then, another statement in cultural terms of that awareness of the reality of community life which we have already noted as growing up in the eighteenth century. Far from being simply one unit of humanity, each actual human being speaks a particular language, has a special religion, wears clothes of a distinct style, and is skilled in activities which compose a particular way of life. Where did these words, beliefs, styles and skills come from? Certainly they were not produced by some faculty like reason. They are the unselfconscious and undesigned products of an encounter between a unique set of people and a changing environment. The only realistic way to see a human being is to recognise him as the inheritor of such a background.

Herder brought a new set of questions to social and political matters. The rationalists of the Enlightenment would ask such questions as: How can we classify this thing? Is it rational? Is it better or worse? Can we prevent it or bring it about? The outcome of such an attitude was a kind of grading process in which, for example, the British Constitution was awarded an alpha, whilst the entire culture of the Middle Ages was relegated to the gamma class. The spread of Enlightenment became a process by which all Europe was to be equipped with alpha-institutions and an alpha-culture. Herder loathed this attitude and he invented many of the charges we still bring against rationalism: that it is uncreative, coldly critical, mechanical, that it fails to understand social phenomena as responses to concrete situations. The question that Herder asked was the historical one: How did this thing come to be what it is? Given this sympathetic approach, we shall no longer be prone to condemn 'ancient Egyptians or mediaeval Englishmen for not being Greeks of the fifth century B.C. and youthful tribes for not behaving like polished Frenchmen of the *grand siècle*. . . . In its time, in its place Oriental despotism was an answer to the needs of young, tender humanity for fatherly protection, and was brought into being by the same sentiments of trust, devotion and awe, that went out to an omnipotent deity. Those who sneer at founders of religions, calling them impostors, or grow eloquent on the evil cunning of Oriental despots, simply lack the imagination to understand the mainsprings of young nations.'[9] This is a view which avoids Scylla only to go crashing into Charybdis. In demanding the sympathy of historical imagination for each culture, it seems to involve a historical relativism which would forbid us to discriminate between, say, science and witchcraft since both are equally and essentially the products of historical causes. Valid in the writing of history, this assumption is stultifying elsewhere.

Herder not only believed that language was the essential attribute of each *Volk*, he approved of the resulting divisions of mankind. The variety of languages cut men off from each other, forcing them into developing their own unique cultures and protecting them from much of the corruption that arises, Herder believed, from imitating foreigners. In these beliefs, he was distinctly an innovator. The one thing that priest and *philosophe* might agree upon across the barricades was their common dismay that the human race spoke numberless languages and dialects. The priest believed this condition to be the result of God's curse upon human presumption in building the Tower of Babel. The *philosophe* regretted the waste, frustration and confusion attendant upon the difficulties of communication between peoples; like all rational men, he yearned for a world language— either a widely current one, like Latin or French or, if that should prove intolerable to nationalist sentiment, then an artificial language like Esperanto. Herder, of course, could not regard such artificial constructions as languages at all. A language expressed a nation's soul or spirit. It was an organic growth which bore the marks of generations of experience, a kind of coded history of the sufferings and joys of the nation. Even the structure of a language seemed to Herder a mirror of the moral character of the people: active peoples, he thought, prefer active verbs. 'We Germans', he wrote in 1787, 'still do not understand the importance of a national language. The bulk of our people still think of it as something that only concerns the grammarian. To consider it as the *organ of social activity and co-operation*, as the bond of social classes and a means for their integration: this is something of which most of us have only the remotest notion.'[10]

The striking thing is that Herder takes language to be 'the bond of social classes'. Political philosophers have more commonly taken some economic or political criterion—interchange of skills, submission to a sovereign, or participation in the market—as the social 'bond'. But given that the essential bond was language, then Herder's Germany was in danger of dissolution. He believed that German culture in his lifetime had become dependent upon the French, whose influence had driven a divisive wedge separating German princely courts from the German people. The political implications of Herder's concern with language are potentially revolutionary. The lower orders are seen as being not simply primitive peasants but as a source of national creativity; language is something which they share equally with the members of the aristocracy, yet in the contemporary situation, the aristocracy was betraying the community's trust by imitating foreign models.

A possible conclusion, therefore, is that salvation must come from below. It is the lower orders who will defend the purity of the language. The indispensability of maintaining purity follows from

Herder's belief that a *Volk* that abandons its language destroys its 'self', that is to say, its people lose their main contact with reality and become mere imitations of foreign models, lost to all vitality, spontaneity and identity. Here was a metaphysical nightmare from which men might only be saved by resolute political action—of the kind Fichte was to suggest in *The Closed Commercial State*. Burke had defended prejudice on the grounds that it was a kind of emotional knowledge deriving from the traditions of society, by contrast with which reason was abstract, flashy, superficial, likely to mislead. Herder similarly admired the role of prejudice in human affairs; he considered that it was the main force which kept nations separate from each other, and consequently pure and authentic. Like all things which divided men from each other, it was a barrier against our becoming cosmopolitans 'like the slaves and the Jews'.[11]

The next generation of German nationalists found all this highly attractive; they refined the argument one further stage. They asserted that of all the nations of Europe, only the Germans had succeeded in maintaining a pure language from their origins to the present day. The unfortunate British and French spoke impure tongues compounded of Latin and German elements; and having thus abandoned purity, they had forsaken their creativity. As Arndt wrote, stating the essence of the nationalist doctrine of the *Volk*: 'All great things which a man does, forms, thinks, and invents as a hero, an artist, a lawgiver, or an inventor—all that comes to him only from the nation.'[12] And the purer the nation and the national language, the greater the things. In Herder, the passion to compare and rank is comparatively absent; he respects on equal terms all peoples, languages, cultures. Herder believed that authenticity alone was valuable. His successors believe that some are more authentic than others. And the proof of authenticity comes to be military power.

Herder's nationalism remained for the most part free of political views, perhaps because in a world wherein there is very little communication between peoples, the vitality of a culture may safely be left to nature combined with a little preaching and exhortation such as that which Herder himself supplies. It becomes very different when one language has possession of an increasing number of highly desirable professional opportunities. In such a situation, a whole culture may find itself on the verge of becoming extinct—as happened in the case of the Celtic and Basque cultures in France and the British Isles. A similar situation arose on Herder's doorstep when Joseph II attempted to give professional advantages to German within Austria-Hungary; this provoked Herder into stating the politics already intimated in his views on language and society: 'The most natural State is a community with its own national character.'[13] He attacked multi-national states as artificial contrivances—'patched-up fragile contractions . . . devoid of inner life'. He could not, in other words, imagine a patriotism that was not nationalist.

Herder is conventionally taken to be part of the romantic movement which was in his lifetime beginning to affect many fields of human activity. One convenient formula we may use in describing romanticism is that it shifted attention away from *external* rules to *inner* spontaneity. In the field of religion, this meant a greater pre-occupation with mystical experiences than with creeds and dogmas. In artistic judgment, it involved admiring spontaneity rather than what conformed to classical rules of proper poetic or aesthetic form.

There is a parallel to this process in the ethics of Herder's contemporary Immanuel Kant, whom no one would wish to call a romantic thinker. Kant's concept of the categorical imperative was a rationalisation of good behaviour which rejected conformity to externally imposed moral rules, in favour of rational inner conviction. Kant argued that the free man was essentially autonomous or self-determined. The 'self' that concerned Kant was that of a rational person, but this limitation was not essential to his theory. A similar autonomy might in similar terms be claimed for other 'selves' or moral entities, such as the nation or *Volk*. 'Nationalism', as Elie Kedourie has argued, 'which is itself . . . largely a doctrine of national self-determination, found here the great source of its vitality.'[14] The form of Kant and the content of Herder might be combined in a fully developed nationalism.

Fichte and the German Nation

It was Napoleon's defeat of the Prussian army at Jena in 1806 which made German nationalism noisy and explicit. It is commonly observed as ironic that Hegel carried the proof sheets of the *Philosophie des Rechts* through the streets of Jena filled with refugees; and on seeing Napoleon he thought, he said later, that he had seen 'the world-soul on horseback'. Hegel's thought is concerned not with the nation but with the state; like Goethe and many other prominent Germans of the time, he was a Francophile. There were others, however, who felt that not merely Prussia but all Germany had been humiliated by Napoleon's triumph. They spoke in terms of German patriotism, and tried to ignore the fact that the Germany they spoke of did not exist. Germany was a cultural and geographical expression, which could lay claim to the historical traditions of the Holy Roman Empire. Napoleon abolished the Holy Roman Empire in 1806, but the Hapsburg Emperor remained the obvious candidate for the leadership of a united Germany. He ruled a heterogeneous realm in which his Germans were a minority among his subjects. The remainder of Germany was ruled despotically by a collection of princes; they were the only political powers in Germany and their interests were directly opposed to German unification. Among these rulers, the Prussian house of Hohenzollern had succeeded in forcing its way into the ranks of the Great Powers and thereby arrived at a certain eminence among the princes. But Prussia itself seemed but a partly German state, situated on the eastern extremes of Germany, ruling over many Slav subjects, and only a marginal participant in the German traditions to which the nationalists looked.

Such was the situation which faced the nationalists after the battle of Jena. In the best intellectual manner, they pretended that these difficulties did not exist. German nationalism thus began in a rhetorical fantasy in which the use of a philosophical vocabulary purporting to describe a 'deeper' reality evaded the more stringent requirements of the workaday world. It was dependent very largely on the unstable enthusiasms of students and teachers, and it made up in polemical violence for its political ineffectiveness. In later years, the period from 1806 to 1813 when Napoleon's forces were driven out of Germany became material for a legend. 'On the outbreak of war in 1813', as A.J.P. Taylor writes, 'Fichte dramatically suspended his lectures "until the liberation of the fatherland". But his only contribution to this liberation was to retire to his study, there to experience sensations of enthusiasm; and the only contribution of German nationalism was to give the battle of Leipzig the romantic name of the "battle of the nations". In fact, no nations fought at Leipzig, only the professional armies of the old order on one side and the polyglot conscripts of the French Emperor on the other.'[15]

Fichte's idea of the nation, though it drew on Herder's opinions, was entirely political. He took over from the French the doctrine that the world has been geographically constructed to accommodate nation-states: 'Certain parts of the earth's surface, together with their inhabitants, are visibly destined by nature to form political entities.'[16] This has been a common nationalist doctrine ever since, whenever convenience has suggested its use. Mazzini, for example, held that God had been especially explicit in laying out Italy as a nation. The French found this doctrine convenient because their obvious frontiers —the Pyrenees, the Alps and the Rhine—enclosed a wider area than was actually inhabited by Frenchmen: 'Nature' appeared to have given the French a large slice of Germany. For Fichte's purposes, the doctrine of natural frontiers needed adaptation, because the Germans inhabited a relatively featureless plain in the centre of Europe. His solution was to develop Herder's cultural nationalism into a doctrine of 'inner frontiers'. 'Those who speak the same language', he wrote, 'are linked together, before human intervention takes a hand, by mere nature with a host of invisible ties; they understand each other and are capable of communicating more and more closely with one another, they belong together, they are by nature one indivisible whole.'[17]

This hardly describes Germany, which, whatever its metaphysical unity 'by nature' and 'before human intervention', had proved far from indivisible politically. The utility of such metaphysical remarks is that they serve as springboards for political dreaming. In fact, Fichte was *advocating* the state of affairs which he asserted already existed *by nature*. It is a common practice in some political writing to use philosophical language to assert that what is politically false is, in some 'higher' sense, true.

Fichte shared Herder's admiration for the role of prejudice in keeping the nation pure, but lacked his faith in its efficacy. He proposed stronger measures to keep the nation sealed off from

foreigners. In *The Closed Commercial State* he outlined an austere
utopia. 'Only the scholar and the creative artist', he wrote with a bow
to the Enlightenment doctrines he had held, 'have reason to travel
outside the closed state. Foreign trade should no longer be permitted
for those who feel merely a leisured curiosity and a desire for
diversion to carry their boredom about through all lands.'[18] It might
appear from such sentiments that Fichte sought to turn his back
upon the rest of the world in order that Germans might cultivate their
own garden. The curious thing about the *Addresses to the German
Nation* is on the contrary their extreme, indeed morbid, sensitivity
to the opinions of foreigners. These *Addresses* are among the earliest
manifestoes of German nationalism, and were delivered as lectures at
the university of Berlin in 1807–8. The audience was not large, and
indeed was partly composed of French officers; but in written form
they have attained a kind of classic status. Fichte commonly talks of
the 'eyes of foreign nations', a metaphor conjuring up a vision of
hostile presences across the frontier.

He uses this metaphor to reinforce his castigation of the Germans
for past faults, a process of self-criticism which came to be a standard
feature of nationalist thinking. 'It is a disgrace in which we Germans
stand alone amidst all the other European nations, who in all other
respects have suffered a like fate, that we are the only nation which,
as soon as foreign arms ruled over us, started ourselves to abuse our
governments, our rulers, whom we had flattered before in a disgust-
ing manner, and everything belonging to our country, as if we had
merely been awaiting this moment and now wished to carry out a
good act before the time for it had passed away.' And again he writes:
'Some of us already at an earlier stage made ourselves completely
contemptible, ridiculous and repulsive by offering on every occasion
the most abject praise to those who were formerly in power in our
country.'[19] And in a within-the-family appeal to preserve face before
the neighbours, he adds characteristically: 'Do we now want to make
foreign nations witnesses of this low disease as well as of the great
gracelessness with which we bestow flattery, so that we may add to
their contempt of our baseness also the ridiculous sight of our
gracelessness?'

These are violent words, and they are entirely general in their application. We may infer, I think, that Fichte was thinking of particular examples, and is here implicitly conducting that spiritual civil war which is always present, indeed a primary element, in nationalism. Fichte has an elevated notion of what it is to be German, and his fury at those Germans who do not act in this manner will be proportionate to the elevation. We may even go further than this. A nationalist claims considerable superiority for the nation he is promoting; but all such claims are inevitably unrealistic. Nationalists are therefore liable to violent alternations of love in contemplating the ideal virtues and hate when they contemplate the actual behaviour of their compatriots. Fichte exhibits this type of alternation.

The particular vices Fichte attributes to the Germans turn out to be the obverse of their virtues. If 'foreign cunning easily outmatched German simplicity and credulity', was this not because the Germans are 'honest, serious, sober' and speak 'a language which is shaped to express the truth'?[20] They are easily influenced and have been corrupted by Gallic cosmopolitanism. The denigration is of a subtle kind, since the simplicity Fichte attacks can be seen in other contexts as a virtue. A dramatic structure emerges from the *Addresses*. Foreigners 'found German valour useful for waging their wars, and German hands useful for seizing loot from their rivals. It was these other countries who first made use of the division of opinions which had arisen in Germany on account of the religious controversies, in order to divide artificially this representative microcosm of the whole of Christian Europe, from being an innate organic unit, into separate independent parts. . . .'[21]

Germans have been, Fichte encourages us to conclude, the victims of foreign cunning. German virtues are natural, German vices the consequences of admitting foreign influences. It is rather like Cinderella exploited by the ugly sisters until the moment of release when her natural beauty and simple goodness triumph. In nationalist thought, the main characteristic of foreigners, apart from malice, is their considerable cunning, a necessary postulate if the currently depressed state of the nation is to be explained. In a milder form, this version of events is found in the British view that aggressors in international relations generally win the first round, and always lose the last. In Fichte and other nationalist writers we may discern a perfectly general fantasy whose mainspring is pleasure at the thought of a suffering hero's triumph. The structure of this fantasy is perfectly general; Fichte casts the French as villains, but according to contemporary or later taste, Jews, aristocrats, the British, or anyone else to hand may be substituted as oppressors of the nation. Indeed one of the striking things about German nationalism is how continuous was this pleasure. In 1895, the nationalist historian Treitschke wrote that 'long after the defeat of Napoleon, in the eyes of foreigners we [Germans] were only the comic-looking, jovial members of singing and shooting clubs, and the German word *Vaterland* was, in England, simply a term of contempt.'[22] Germany had at this time long been recognised as the strongest military power on the Continent, and his message clearly reads: they used to laugh at us, but they don't any more. It certainly seems plausible to suggest that one of the causes of German nationalism's consistent concern with power is a fear of looking ridiculous; men do not laugh at those they fear.

Much nationalist writing takes the form of such fantasy structures. This is particularly clear in the case of Arndt, who lacked Fichte's philosophical abilities. In 1813 he wrote: 'I have known misfortunes; I have suffered; it has scarcely moved me to tears. But when I have thought of the *Volk* I have always had to weep in the depth of my soul. When a great crowd moves before me, when a band of warriors passes by with flowing banners and sounding trumpets and drums, then I realise that my feelings and my actions are not an empty illusion, then it is that I feel the indestructible life, the eternal spirit, and eternal God. . . . Like other men I am egoistic and sinful but in my exaltation I am freed at once from all my sins, I am no longer a single suffering individual, I am one with the *Volk*, and God. In such a moment any doubts about my life and work vanish.'[23] Now what Arndt here presents as admirable is the contrast between ordinary sinful egoism and the noble call to duty when the nation calls. But this is a parody of virtue, for it is in fact an abdication of individual responsibility. The *Volk* is a fantasy, especially in Arndt's time when there did not exist a German state to which the fantasy might be attached. It is a fantasy connected with military force, but this military force is conceived of primarily in sentimental terms— warriors, trumpets, banners waving in the wind. Arndt is moved by

symbols, not by concrete experiences, and he exhorts his compatriots to a similar emotion: 'German, feel again God, hear and fear
the eternal, and you hear and fear also your *Volk*; you feel again in
God the honour and dignity of your fathers, their glorious history
rejuvenates itself again in you, their firm and gallant virtue reblossoms
in you, the whole German Fatherland stands again before you in the
august halo of past centuries!'[24] It is passages like this which make it
plausible to suggest that nationalism is a form of religious life, for
Arndt is clearly trying to associate God and the nation, and perhaps
indeed has mixed them up in his own mind.

   The next best thing to the fantasy being realised is to imagine that
it has been. Arndt writes of 1813: 'Fired with enthusiasm, the people
rose, "with God for King and Fatherland". Among the Prussians
there was only one voice, one feeling, one anger and one love, to save
the Fatherland and to free Germany.' The spring behind this rhetoric
is a hatred of individuality, a passion to lose oneself in a single
communal emotion. Arndt presents us with a picture rather like
Michelet's account of the French Revolution. He writes: 'The most
beautiful thing about all this holy zeal and happy confusion was that
all differences of position, class, and age were forgotten . . . that the
one great feeling for the Fatherland, its freedom and honour,
swallowed all other feelings, caused all other considerations and
relationships to be forgotten.'[25]

   The reality was, as we have observed, quite different. Certainly the
King of Prussia had no patience with this kind of thing, and appealed
to his subjects in measured and local terms. The French had no
trouble with guerrilla units in Germany such as they had to meet in
Spain and Russia. In 1813, largely under the influence of Friedrich
Jahn, a few thousand patriotic volunteers were enlisted as the Free
Corps, and fought at the Battle of Leipzig: militarily an insignificant
element among the 300,000 conscripts of the Prussian army. Jahn
was one of the earliest nationalists to believe that Prussia rather than
Austria was the 'kernel' of a divided Germany. He was the first of a
long line of enthusiasts who organised German youth into activities
dedicated to some version of the national cause. Jahn led his students
in gymnastic exercises whose purpose was to strengthen their will in
preparation for the day of national liberation. He was the leading

spirit in the formation of the *Burschenschaft* or student societies who raised the black, red and gold colour as the flag of German unity.

They burnt books and made demonstrations. Once they went so far as to engage in assassination—in 1819, when Carl Sand shot the dramatist Kotzebue. But it did not add up to a national ferment. The German nationalists of this period found themselves sandwiched between a passive population and a hostile set of rulers; it was like trying to set fire to the sea. Only a few of that generation were to survive to 1871, to enjoy a senile satisfaction at the military triumph which looked like the realisation of their dreams.

Problems of German Nationalism

On 18 January 1871, at Versailles in the heart of defeated France, King William I of Prussia was proclaimed Emperor. If the aim of nationalism is to achieve unity and self-determination, then the Germans seemed to have arrived. According to the model we suggested in Chapter 1, German politics should then have settled down to consolidate this unity, and nationalist issues should have played a declining part in political life. Up to a point this did happen. The growing Social Democratic party devoted itself to the class struggle, and sought benefits for the trade unions. The Centre Party defended Catholic interests in the new *Reich*. An extraordinarily rapid process of industrialisation absorbed much German energy. The passion of German nationalists, however, came in time to intensify rather than to abate. Quite new ideas were developed. Whilst Bismarck remained in power, this ferment was kept in check. After he was forced from office in 1890, it was free to cooperate with the ambitions of the young Kaiser. The Kaiser saw himself as a kind of sun-king and sought dynastic expansion on the world political stage. Nationalist ideas filtered into new social channels, infecting Germans in Austria-Hungary, promoting dissatisfaction with existing frontiers, and causing dreams of impossible glory.

We are today likely to see these events through a haze compounded of the First and Second World Wars, and the Nazi period. It looks, in this perspective, as if we may speak of a continuous nationalism running from 1806 to 1945. Such a vision leads us to an almost automatic prejudice against German nationalism. It also leads to some pretty brutal simplification. Here is one example: 'National unity came late to Germany but with potent force. Nationalism became more and more aggressive in the Wilhelmian era. In the Nazi period, under a monomaniacal *Führer*, it went berserk. The warning came in *Mein Kampf*: "It is clear that everything must be subordinated to the nation's interest." Even human decency! The Nazi Third *Reich* marked Western civilisation at its nadir.'[26]

Our initial problem, then, is to try and discover why a group of people who said they were dissatisfied because something had not happened, remained dissatisfied after it had. And the answer lies, initially, in keeping clear in our minds the difference between the top and bottom of the German political hierarchy. Although for most of the nineteenth century German nationalism was a middle-class movement, it looked forward to a spontaneous movement from below of an enthusiastic German populace. The attempt to unify Germany in this manner had failed most conspicuously in 1848–9. At that time, the National Assembly at Frankfurt had tried to exercise power over all Germany. Looking to Austria for support, it had chosen the Hapsburg Archduke John as its prince. Its chance had come when revolution temporarily paralysed both Vienna and Berlin. It was dominated by liberals aiming at a federal Germany whose political system would be a constitutional monarchy. It failed, however, to sustain its power, or even to remain true to its nationalist principles. German nationalists failed the test of principle when they applauded, in the name of 'healthy national egoism', the Austrian suppression of the Czechs. Times and temper had changed since Herder's respect for the equality of nations. Like most nationalist bodies, the National Assembly could not contemplate any surrender of territory in the name of nationalist principles. In 1849, as its ineffectuality was becoming evident, and Berlin and Vienna asserted their former sway, the Assembly sent a deputation to Berlin to offer the Imperial Crown to Frederick William IV of Prussia. On the advice of his ministers, he replied that he 'would not pick up a Crown from the gutter'. He would, in other words, only accept such a Crown from the German princes, who were far from prepared to surrender their power. 1849 was, then, a failure for liberal nationalism.

The actual unification of Germany came from the 'top'. The process began in 1862 when Bismarck became Chancellor of Prussia and within ten years waged the three rapid and successful wars against Denmark, Austria and France which resulted in a unified Germany under Prussian hegemony. It was not that Germany had absorbed Prussia, but that Prussia had taken over Germany—and on Prussia's terms.

Germany had thus been unified not 'from below' but rather 'from above'. And whilst the policy of the Prussian rulers coincided up to a point with that of German nationalists—both were expansionist, for example—they were fundamentally distinct. Bismarck thought in dynastic terms; he continued the policy of Frederick the Great and thought always as a Prussian. The nationalists looked to the creation of a German nation-state which would unite all Germans scattered through central Europe; it would involve rule over the Slav peoples who lived among them. The Prussian policy was to maintain Austria intact—and Bismarck had been very careful to maintain her territorial integrity after Prussia's defeat of her in 1866. The German nationalists, on the other hand, recognised as the logic of their policy that the Austrian Empire must be broken up.

In spite of these divergences, many German nationalists were happy to applaud Bismarck's success. Few can resist patriotic enthusiasm; and it is even harder to keep a clear head in the face of patriotic victories. A common charge made against German nationalism is that at each crisis in its affairs, it capitulated to military success, caring more for power than for its ideals. The Prussian parliament, for example, in 1866 indemnified the victorious Bismarck against four years of unconstitutional behaviour. And in 1871, the majority of German nationalists were sufficiently carried away by a victory over the traditional enemy, France, to acquiesce in a Prussian-dominated *Reich* which was far from their federal hopes. Some, however, resisted. In the Bavarian legislature, 48 members, for example, voted against ratifying the Treaty of Versailles in 1871. But most were able to find a way of discovering that it was their duty to support the new dispensation.[27]

The characteristic vice of a civilisation that justifies its actions in terms of duty is that of hypocrisy. Those who consistently claim that duty leads in the same direction as aggrandisement of power are extremely vulnerable to this charge. The idea of duty promiscuously consorting with that of conquest may be typically seen in the historian Theodor Mommsen in defending the Prussian annexation of his own province of Schleswig-Holstein. 'Our South German friends', he wrote in 1865, 'speak of the Prussian lust for conquest, but anyone who knows the Prussians knows that we cannot speak of their lustful conquest but only of duty. . . . If the great dream of 1848 [for German unity] should come true, then every means, including force, will be justified. Necessity and the nation both speak in the categorical imperative, and as the nation-state can heal every wound, it is also entitled to inflict every wound.'[28] In Mommsen's case, our charge must be mental confusion rather than hypocrisy, for he was later to be conspicuous as one of what Hans Kohn calls the 'disillusioned voices', those who expressed their disenchantment with Bismarck's Germany. But the general effect of elevated and pseudo-philosophical sentiments of this kind has been to add self-righteousness to the ordinary conflicts of international relations.

It is possible, then, to argue that the policy of Germans was always the attainment of power, and that in 1871 this passion sought merely new areas to conquer. But an alternative view might be that, on arriving at nationhood, Germans discovered themselves in a quite new situation. For one thing, there remained many Germans outside the state; 1871, therefore, looked merely like no more than a stage on the way to a Greater Germany. For another thing, Germany found herself in a peculiarly perilous position. She was surrounded by potential enemies—by the Russians, with advantages in land and men; by the French, whose politics now came to be dominated by the thirst for revenge and recapture of Alsace-Lorraine; by the British, as guardians of the international *status quo*. And, from a nationalist point of view, there was the fact that in the period when Germany was becoming unified, the leading nations had significantly changed the idea of what it was to be a great nation: they had colonised large tracts of the world. Germany had reached the European stage only to discover that Europe no longer counted as it had.

Here, then, were problems facing German nationalism after unification. The manner in which these problems were considered was characteristic of nationalist thinking. It is common among politicians to make long-range forecasts, partly for amusement, and partly as a basis for policy. These forecasts are usually concerned with the future strength of states and their likely development. Such disparate figures as de Tocqueville and Bismarck both predicted that America and Russia would dominate the politics of the twentieth century because of their size. Thinking in this manner had earlier been confined to the tiny class of the politically engaged. Now, with the growth of literacy and intellectuality, whole new classes engaged in it. It became a common feature of nationalist thought. Nationalism turned it into a kind of philosophy of history—but the sort of history no one can write because it concerns future events. Nationalists forecast the destinies, not of states, but of peoples, civilisations, nations. They used the vocabulary of national missions. And one common conclusion reached by Germans towards the end of the nineteenth century was that Germany, as the predominant land power of the world, was destined to clash with the predominant sea power, England, the guardian of the existing distribution of world power.

This issue became mixed up with another, the solution of which is crucial to nationalism. It is the problem of national identity—no problem for states but crucial for nations. Germany was culturally and geographically intermediate between, on one side, the Latin and Anglo-Saxon West and, on the other side, the increasingly self-conscious mass of Slavs. We have already seen that in the war against Napoleon, German nationalists had rejected all things French. But German nationalism had an inescapably metaphysical cast of mind which led it continually into higher realms of abstraction. Just as Napoleon and the *philosophes* 'stood for' France, so France might be taken to 'stand for' something even more abstract—'the West' perhaps, or even 'civilisation', which might all be dismissed as 'superficial' and 'mechanical' by contrast with the organic and profound character of German 'culture'. France stood for a collection of ideas which had to be rejected in the name of German patriotism: liberalism, the emancipation of the Jews, individualism, classicism. This was a strand of German nationalism which persisted through the nineteenth century and developed new ramifications in the period after 1870.

This formulation of the problem of national identity was adopted on the Continent wherever German philosophy became influential—in such countries as Russia and Spain. They faced an even more severe problem of national identity—a foretaste of the situation of 'underdeveloped' countries in the twentieth century. The Germans pioneered what has become the standard reaction: they asserted a spiritual superiority, a superiority in terms of depth of culture, to contrast with the mechanised barbarism they chose to see in the West.

In both Russia and Spain, the debate was a matter not only of national identity, but also one of policy. Should these countries hasten to industrialise and catch up with the West, or should they, at considerable cost in terms of power, retain what they considered was a unique spiritual heritage. In Germany, the question of policy was rapidly outflanked by events; the country was in the midst of a rapid industrialisation. But faith in cultural superiority could still be used to identify Germany's mission in the future struggles so commonly predicted.

The German military staff always suffered from the nightmare of having to fight a war on two fronts. German nationalist intellectuals lived with this nightmare continually. For when they looked west, they felt, perhaps a little uneasily, that they were culturally superior; but on looking to the east they found their superiority in supposedly Western qualities like efficiency. In one mood, Germans would (like Thomas Mann during the First World War) consider themselves spiritually linked to the Russians; in another mood (one which prevailed after 1917) they would regard themselves as the defenders of Western civilisation against the Barbarous Bolshevik. The Teutonic Knights were always held in readiness to ride again. Both German nationalists and their enemies made use of the old Roman frontier which had divided the Germanic tribes from the civilisation of Imperial Rome. It was taken as an eternal frontier of the European spirit. But what the frontier signified was determined by politics, not history.

The problem of national identity was intensified by rapid industrialisation. Germany was changing, and nationalists mostly disliked the direction of the change. Nothing promotes an appreciation of Nature more than urban growth. German nationalists believed that urban growth was something positively evil—an alienation from the countryside and from the rural virtue which was specifically German.[29] One modification of nationalist theory which developed around this period was that the national soul was a reflection of the national landscape. The Jews, it was thought, had shallow and arid souls because their spiritual composition had been determined by life in the desert. The Germans, living in dark, mist-shrouded forests, were deep, mysterious and profound.[30] We may well sympathise with the anxieties of anyone who believed this, and saw his countrymen increasingly immured in sunless slums.

The nationalists now saw two Germanies: there was the traditional Germany made up of selected elements from the German past combined with hopes for the German future. And there was modern Germany, a place of cities and bustling industry which in its greed, competitiveness and lack of respect for tradition was indistinguishable from any other capitalist country. In other words, they found themselves intellectually in the same situation as their predecessors of the Napoleonic generation, with the slight difference that the enemy was no longer France but capitalism. At this stage, nationalism became selfconsciously quaint—with folk dancing and *Lederhosen*—and encouraged superficial national differentiation for which the tourist industry later supplied new motives.

In the 1890s this contrast dominated the thought of nationalists all over Europe, adding a new dimension to the problem of national identity. In all countries it produced a good deal of reflection on the new phenomenon of the masses. The masses were those who lived in cities: the crowd, the herd, thoughtless, easily led, fickle, a force vulgarising culture and debasing morality. The idea of the masses has as its correlative the notion of a smaller, superior group, which was most commonly called the élite, but could appear under other names such as the superman, the natural aristocracy, the sensitive, or the discriminating. This structure had any number of ramifications —from André Gide's *acte gratuit* which purports to be motiveless and therefore free and élitist, to Nietzsche's *Übermensch*. But the nationalists, forsaking Herder's faith in popular simplicity, tended to introduce élite–mass terminology into the familiar contrast between the national purity and cosmopolitan superficiality.

As a formal structure, the theory of élites and masses may be put to almost any use that may be required. Everything depends upon how one identifies the two components of the theory. It might seem, for example, that the despised masses must be the proletariat, and that the theory must be anti-socialist. But this is not so. Socialists were able to adapt it to their use. In France Georges Sorel with largely Marxist assumptions identified the bourgeoisie as the masses, consumptionist and utilitarian, and attributed the heroic virtues of the élite to the proletariat. In this form, the doctrine influenced Mussolini and with further modifications became part of the official ideology of Italian fascism. The élite might, and in Germany did, get mixed up with Eastern notions of spiritually superior people, and thus become a vehicle for theosophical ideas.[31] In this form it was to play a part in the generation of Nazism. Élites and masses might be identified according to choice, but the theory was not entirely neutral in its political consequences. Anyone who used them was certain to cast himself as part of the élite; and the doctrine at this period was invariably anti-capitalist. It was a doctrine generally used defensively by people who thought that their side had been, at least for the moment, defeated. It is often characterised as irrationalist, since it commonly contrasted the beauties of intuition or some higher faculty of knowledge with the 'mechanical' operations of a superficial rationality. And above all, it was violently hostile to democracy, the doctrine which was held responsible for the disastrous triumph of the masses.

Nationalists, then, thought in terms of masses and élites in their hatred of capitalist modernity, a new version of the hatred of the West which had been part of German thought since Fichte's generation. And in the minds of most German nationalists, a hatred of capitalism and democracy was inescapably linked to a hatred of the Jews. The very presence of the Jews and their prominence in German economic life was to be attributed to their emancipation which had been a consequence of the French Revolution and of Enlightenment doctrines. In a regionally and socially divided Germany, the Jews stood out as the symbol of a social element which was radically unassimilable, since it had maintained a separate identity in hostile surroundings for over 2,000 years. German nationalists were prone to remark that 'the Jews are our misfortune'. But German anti-Semitism is not an easy thing to evaluate. For one thing, it was subject to the metaphysical tendencies of all German thinking; the Jews therefore were hated as 'manifestations' of commercial principles, as well as being concretely disliked. A man like the theologian Paul de Lagarde, one of those to whom the phrase about the Jews being a misfortune is attributed, believed that the Jews were a *cultural* impediment to the unity of Germany, and was perfectly capable of despising those who based their anti-Semitism on *racial* grounds.[32] He is recorded as having been helpful to several Jewish students. Richard Wagner, whose music was the centre of a considerable ideological industry, also expressed violent anti-Semitic sentiments. 'I have cherished a long repressed resentment of this Jew business', he wrote to Liszt in 1851, 'and this grudge is as necessary to my nature as gall is to the blood.'[33] Yet he accepted Jewish admirers and worked with them. A Russian-Jewish pianist called Joseph Rubenstein lived in his house from 1872 until the composer's death, after which in 1884 he committed suicide, unable, it is said, to envisage life without the master.[34]

The case of German nationalist anti-Semitism faces us with a common problem in the study of nationalist ideas. These ideas are usually collections of metaphysical abstractions which have no *necessary* connection with the flesh and blood of here and now. They are often only to be taken as forms of self-expression; records, as we argued earlier, of political fantasies rather than statements of policy. But it is clear that this was not always the case, for the anti-Semitism was perfectly real and, under Nazi rule, anti-Semitic attitudes were insanely carried over into political practice. Possibly because of its wider social diffusion, German nationalism after 1871 lost its former coherence and broke up into a spectrum of different obsessions.

The spectrum runs from infra-refined to ultra-vulgar; from the highminded idealism of Paul de Lagarde, and even the traditionalism of Treitschke at one end to the rasping anti-Semitism and greedy ambition of the streets at the other. Between the two extremes, we find nature-worship, novel Germanic theologies, nudism, nationalist mysticism, cyclical philosophies of history, racial anthropology, even the operatic nationalism of Richard Wagner. Small private groups of intellectuals, utopian communities, political cells, student fraternities, walking associations, and coffee-house gatherings cultivated such ideas. An account of nationalism in this period degenerates into a list because of its overwhelming variety. The ranks of nationalists were being augmented, especially among Austrian Germans, by masses of comparatively little men who chose nationalism rather than socialism as the vehicle of their political assertiveness. Traditionally nationalist groups such as schoolteachers were changing their tone in reaction to a commercial Germany where they thought respect for learning and quality was disappearing. They called for discipline and a return to the old hierarchy; and when men call for discipline, they are not usually asking to be disciplined; and when they regret the absence of hierarchy, it is generally not the shortage of superiors they feel so much as the absence of inferiors. These were new elements, both intellectual and sociological, in nationalism, and they were in time to transform it into something different. The slogans, often retained from the past, conveyed new meanings to their adherents.

It would be tidy if we could simply make a distinction between highminded traditional nationalism and the racism of the mob. The former might be seen culminating in the 20 July plot against Hitler in 1944, the latter in Nazism itself. But it was not like that. Why it wasn't can be illustrated by the case of Lagarde, who in all the obvious ways belongs to the top end of the spectrum. Lagarde yearned for a morally purified Germany; his has been called 'the politics of cultural despair'. 'Through politics', Fritz Stern argues, Lagarde 'sought to gain spiritual ends, to reach and transform the moral life of man.'[35] Lagarde's anti-Semitism, we have observed, purported to be cultural rather than racial. Yet he was capable of attacking the Jews as 'the carriers of decay' who 'pollute every national culture'. They 'exploit the human and material resources of their hosts, they destroy all faith and spread materialism and liberalism'.[36] A true conspiracy theorist, he believed that Jews and capitalists (whom he frequently identified) had gained control of the universities and the professions; they controlled all thought. And carried away by his theme, he could write: 'With trichinae and bacilli one does not negotiate, nor are trichinae and bacilli subjected to education; they are exterminated as quickly and as thoroughly as possible.' His belief in the national mission of the Germans was, like all such beliefs, expansionist. In Lagarde's case, it carries us right to the edge of nationalism, and beyond into the shadow-land of fascism or 'tribal nationalism'. Lagarde thought that peoples become nations by collective acceptance of a divinely ordained mission. And God had imposed upon the Germans the mission of colonising the non-German lands of the Austrian Empire.

Any attempt to discover a meaning in German nationalism must begin by recognising its paradoxical character. Doctrines point one way, actions point another. Lunacy and logic are entangled with each other like some Laocoön of the mind. Even the most impressive figures have this Jekyll and Hyde character. Lagarde's aspirations were as idealistic as one might find anywhere, but his yearning for a *Führer* or leader to create a morally purified state plays into the hands of all that was worst in German politics. Lagarde is here a special case of the German nationalist hunger for a *good* state, and satisfaction with a *strong* one.

Early German nationalism had been a revolt against external rules, and a turning to spontaneity. But the German who was thus being taught to admire spontaneity was also being taught that the state represented the highest ethical element of his nature. A yearning for spontaneity thus ended in servile obedience to an external agency. In the latter half of the nineteenth century, nationalists attacked the herd-like behaviour of the masses and promoted admiration for the heroic virtues. Yet the outcome of this feeling was obedience to the Kaiser and an abdication of individual criticism. Here we may suspect that the solution of this paradox lies in the fact that a simple dislike of weakness had been superficially moralised into an idealistic love of heroism; the ethical component was not so much window-dressing as mental confusion. And the time was to come when Hitler would be able to turn virtually the whole German population into a herd by the simple expedient of explaining to them that, racially speaking, they were *all* essentially leaders. He persuaded them that in accepting despotic rulers they were merely taking up their inherited mission as masters.

Perhaps even more fundamentally we may suspect that German nationalism was the result of a dream that had for accidental reasons strayed into politics—the same dream of harmony and communal unity which we have encountered before. That dream had one brief moment of glory, when it imagined that events had cut the Gordian knot of political complexity—August 1914, those 'never-to-be-forgotten days' as Thomas Mann described them. And Adolf Hitler, who was to transform this tradition, wrote of this time: 'For me those hours came as liberation from the oppression that weighed me down so heavily in my youth. I am not ashamed of admitting it, I was overcome by the enthusiasm of the moment. I fell on my knees and thanked the maker of heaven and earth from the depths of my heart for his abundant kindness in giving me a chance to live in such a time.'[37] But for most men, the dream turned out to be the urge to self-destruction.

4

Europe Exports Nationalism

Nationalism and Traditional Societies

We must now turn from the European source of nationalist ideas to their diffusion throughout the non-European world in the twentieth century. And our first impression must be one of the sheer power of nationalism as a movement which has rapidly reversed the nineteenth-century European domination of the world. Compare the ancient with the modern world. Many parts of the Mediterranean were ruled from Rome for 500 or 600 years. European dominion has been very much shorter. The French went into Algeria in 1830 and stayed there till 1962. Their imperial history is entirely contained within that period. The 'scramble for Africa' began in the 1880s, and most Europeans were out of the continent well before a century had passed. Such experiences make Britain's two centuries in India look like a long innings, but two centuries is shortness itself compared with many another empire in the past.

Why such speed? There is no real answer to this question. The best we can do is to accumulate a set of 'factors' which will make it seem less remarkable. We might note that the Roman Empire was not separated from the metropolis by thousands of miles of sea. Further, it was ruled by a succession of emperors, many of whom were themselves provincials. It is hard to imagine a Nigerian as either king or prime minister of Great Britain. The imperial structures of the ancient and modern world were quite different. Again, most Romans never doubted that to become a Roman citizen was a valuable honour. But modern Europeans carried with them the boot that would eventually send them packing—the nationalist belief that anything else but self-government is a kind of slavery. It was often

Europeans themselves who, in the first instance, encouraged the subjects of empire to the exertions which ended all European empires. The Indian National Congress, for example, was founded in 1885 with the approval of the Viceroy, Lord Dufferin, by a Scotsman, Allan Octavian Hume. Hume wrote in his appeal to educated Indians: 'And if amongst you, the *élite*, fifty men cannot be found with sufficient power of self-sacrifice, sufficient love and pride in their country, sufficient genuine and unselfish heart-felt patriotism to take the initiative and, if needs be, devote the rest of their life to the cause—then there is no hope for India. Her sons must and will, remain mere humble and helpless instruments in the hands of foreign rulers, for if "they would be free, *themselves* must strike the blow".'[1] Many other Europeans, of course, held quite different views, and regarded their imperial superiority as a civilising mission likely to last a long time. But even these people promoted the study of such episodes as the English Civil War and the French Revolution from which the colonised peoples could draw conclusions about imperial rule.

If, then, we speed up the events of history, we may see this story in terms of two waves—a wave of colonisation which rapidly dominated the world, and an even more rapid nationalist wave which destroyed European rule in the course of a couple of decades. We may thus be led to the belief (itself part of nationalist ideology) that nationalism is what journalists so commonly call it, 'the strongest force in the modern world'. We may contrast with this a belief held by many opponents of nationalism: that it is merely the work of a few agitators and communists. This anti-nationalist explanation suggests that a fundamentally contented population, which in its rational moments recognises the benefits of European rule, has been stirred up by ambitious politicians. The nationalist explanation suggests that the Afro-Asian masses, awakening to their suffering and exploitation, have risen up to take their political destinies into their own hands. Both these accounts are partial and defective, but it might be useful to keep them in view as we discuss modern nationalism.

One way in which we might pose the problem of this section is to observe that in the century preceding 1945, the most important fact of Afro-Asian political life was that a handful of European soldiers could conquer and control vast territories. The reason is wittily summed up in Hilaire Belloc's couplet:

> *Thank the Lord that we have got*
> *The Gatling gun, and they have not.*

Since 1945, by contrast, the equally dominant fact has been that a handful of guerrillas can hold down large European armies. Why have these abrupt changes in the balance of power come about?

Mention of the Gatling gun suggests a technological theory of imperialism: Europe expanded when it had bullets to fire against bows and arrows; and it contracted once the natives had acquired stocks of rifles and learned how to use them. It is not so much that the Afro-Asian peoples became technologically equal with Europeans. It is rather that machine guns will deal easily with bows and arrows, but it takes very much more expensive equipment to deal with machine guns in the hands of natives organised as a guerrilla or terrorist force. The point will at last come when the game begins to cost more than it is worth, and then imperialism ceases.

But human behaviour is not merely the result of the available tools; it is determined by beliefs and will. How do we explain the success and failure of imperialism in these human terms? The general answer, for what it is worth, would go something like this: Afro-Asian societies used to be governed by traditional rulers. These rulers had a monopoly of political initiative. Once defeated, they came to terms with the Europeans, and their peoples followed suit because no other kind of behaviour, short of desperation, occurred to them. Besides, in many cases the imperialist powers retained the traditional rulers—princes, sultans, chieftains—and contented themselves with installing advisers. For most people, life went on as before, except that mission stations sprang up and there was a chance of making money in the cities.

So much for the success of imperialism. The more complicated question is to discover why it disappeared so rapidly. We may understand this process in terms of a triangle of forces. In the first place there is the traditional social structure in which chiefs and princes rule over a largely rural population. The chiefs may be tribal leaders, as in Africa, or the Sheiks of the Middle East, or the Sultans of the Malay peninsula. In each case, we find a customary world in which social relationships remain static, and the political structure is cemented by an established priesthood. Juxtaposed against this traditional leadership we find the imperialist power, which is often content to leave the traditional rulers more or less in control of their peoples. Sometimes, of course, there are years of fighting between the European power and the established chiefs. The French took decades to subdue Morocco, and the British had to maintain strong forces on the north-west frontier of India. The growth of nationalism depends not upon this tribal resistance but upon the development of a third new social complex composed of Westernised natives.

Typically, the introduction of Western techniques of medicine cuts the death-rate, and population begins to increase rapidly. This creates difficulties which a traditional system of agriculture cannot deal with, and men are therefore driven away from their villages into the cities, mines and plantations which grow up in the wake of Western economic enterprise. Some natives are recruited into a local police force; others are trained as clerks in local government or industry, and thereby become literate. Their situation is transformed in a way difficult for Europeans to understand, for in Europe this transformation has been spread over several centuries. But there is evidence that a new personality structure must come into existence as the result of these economic and social changes. It seems that peasants who live in villages find it extremely difficult to imagine themselves living any other kind of life. Their behaviour is very largely determined by custom; they seldom have to 'make up their minds' on any problem. The village supplies them with a religious belief, and until missionaries turn up, it hardly occurs to them that any other belief is a real possibility. The work they will do and the people they will marry are arranged for them. Asked to imagine the prospect of living somewhere else, they commonly reply that they would rather be dead. The spending of money, which is the exercise of choice, is something with which they are largely unfamiliar. Nor do they have political opinions, for politics is the function of the village chief, who is firmly linked to a hierarchy of obedience. When men leave the villages in which their ancestors have long lived, they move into an unsettling world in which hopes and frustrations take on enormous force. Their minds begin to fill with that enormous baggage we call culture—an awareness of the other countries of the earth, and of the other civilisations which have at various times prospered on it; and an imaginative understanding of people in other places and situations—from Hamlet and Portia to James Bond and Batman.[2]

Such is an absurdly compressed account of the way in which a new social complex comes into being in colonised or semi-colonial territories. It is a summary of sociological theories, themselves a caricature of the many and subtle variations of historical experience. But it supplies us with a peg on which we may hang our account of the emergence of modern nationalism. The new people we have described are the nationalist masses, and we meet them in the newspapers primarily as rioters and guerrilla fighters without individual personalities of their own. They possess their own leaders in the form of an élite who have had the benefits of European education. For at the same time as the peasants are leaving the village and going into the town, a few lucky or pertinacious young men are setting out for the universities of the imperial country. Often they are the sons of the traditional leaders, for, at least in the beginning, only the rich can afford such education. Often it may happen that for several generations, the European-educated are content to operate within a European framework—as lawyers, doctors, civil servants. But the time always comes when this educated élite makes a bid for power, and when it does so, it most commonly uses the rhetoric of nationalism.

Such are the statics of modern nationalism—a structure determined by the relationship between the traditional leaders, the colonial power, and the nationalist élite. There are many ways in which the potential conflict between this triangle of powers may work itself out. One of the commonest outcomes is for the nationalist élite to reduce the traditional leadership to powerlessness—the way the Indian princes were reduced to nullity by the Indian government after 1947, or the way in which Mr Obote of Uganda with a little quick violence in 1966 removed King Freddie, the Kabaka of Buganda, from his throne. But a similar bid for power by Dr Mossadeq in Persia was defeated by the traditional leadership; and a revolution in the Yemen led to a protracted civil war. In Japan the struggle never broke out of the traditional framework, and Japan, far and away the most rapidly and successfully modernised of non-European countries, achieved it entirely within a traditional framework. What is true, however, is that if the traditional leadership is to survive, it must change the basis on which it leads. This transition to modernity requires considerable skill. Prince Sihanouk of Cambodia appears to have made a successful change into President Sihanouk; but King Amanullah of Afghanistan was in 1929 driven from his realm because of his enthusiasm for such changes as female emancipation.

The first question which faces an intelligent traditional leadership is: How much Western culture should be imported? The first thing that intelligent natives want—as the cowboy film constantly reminds us—is guns, for guns were the instruments of their defeat. But even the reception of guns involves a social reorganisation with galloping consequences. The effect of technology even of the simplest kind upon a native culture finds its classic illustration in the reception of steel axes by the Yir Yurout Australian aborigines. The tribe had previously used stone axes made by the men, whose power and prestige rested upon their axe monopoly. With the advent of steel axes, the men of the tribe lost their old place in the culture,[3] and seniority, trade and even religious beliefs were affected. The effects of Western technology are difficult to calculate, and beyond the power of native authorities to control. An almost irresistible early reform introduced by most imperial authorities is modern hygiene, but as we have seen, it is precisely this salutary measure which leads more or less inevitably to a rise in population and the consequent disruption of social structure which sets the country on the path to modernisation.

Conflict between the imperial rulers and the native population is in the end set off by a variety of factors over which neither has very much control. Commonly, natives will put up with a great deal from an imperial administration which seems invincible and convinced of its own righteousness. But in the last century, faith in imperial invincibility has been shaken by a succession of wars. After 1905, when Japan had defeated Russia in Manchuria, it no longer seemed inevitable that Asians *must* be defeated in any military encounter with Western Powers. The two world wars brought it home to colonial subjects that their own particular ruler was by no means the only occupant of the European Olympus, and in 1942 large colonial areas in Asia were overrun by the Japanese. The power of the British, French and Dutch could never look quite the same afterwards. Nor was this simply a matter of measuring native strength against Europeans. The fall of dynasties like the Romanov, the Manchu and the Hohenzollern created a somewhat romantic atmosphere in which almost anything seemed possible.

We may add racialism to these factors. Mostly, Afro-Asian intellectuals were eager to be on the closest terms with their European rulers. Sometimes this desire encountered sympathetic Europeans; far more often it encountered a somewhat chilly benevolence. The actual power relationship of ruler and ruled produced misunderstandings and false assumptions on each side which it would have taken enormous spiritual dexterity to avoid. The classic description of this type of situation is to be found in E. M. Forster's novel *A Passage to India*. Hatreds have a way of generalising; a man who is jilted by one woman often turns into a woman-hater. The course of emotional safety lies in retreating to reliance upon 'one's own' group, and in colonies this group is racially constituted. Bafflements between human beings arising from this type of situation are likely to turn into defensive metaphysics, like Kipling's 'East is East and West is West and never the twain shall meet'.

The Afro-Asian élite, whatever its original ambitions about westernisation, will eventually decide that in the nature of things, Afro-Asians can only be second-class Europeans. All the factors we have been considering lead it towards drawing the obvious conclusion: that it would be better to become first-class Afro-Asians. Whereas one generation is eager to assimilate, the cultural nationalists of the next are already expressing anxiety lest they should be losing their unique African, Indian, Arab, etc., qualities. Such is the psychic history of nationalism.

The use of nationalist doctrine arises within the complex of forces we have already noted. We must remain content to consider a typical situation. Commonly, rivalry grows up between the traditional leadership (in Africa, for example, tribal chiefs) and the energetic young men, back from years of studying abroad, the leaders of the new mass political parties whose strength lies in the towns. To some extent, this is an uncomplicated power struggle: the young Nkrumahs, Obotes, Nehrus, Sukarnos and Nassers are contending for the power and prestige held by the chiefs and sultans. The nationalists want to set up new states which, though modern, will yet not be carbon copies of those in the West. They want to transform politics, and that is why nationalist doctrines are useful to them.

Yet the obvious paradox is that nationalism outside Europe is a sustained exercise in unreality, for there is no nation to start with. The concrete reality of Afro-Asian politics is the caste, the religious community, or the tribe. The competition between the traditional leadership and the nationalist élite is partly a question of what sort of conflict one prefers. The power of tribal chiefs rests upon hostility to other tribes; nationalist politicians serve both their own interests and also those of modernisation by trying to divert animosity away from other tribes towards the imperialist rulers of their countries. In this way, they try not only to rouse a united mass movement, but also to undermine the power of their competitors in the traditional hierarchy. The way in which these aims come together may be illustrated from a typical resolution from the All-African Peoples' Conference held at Accra in 1958: ' . . . we strongly oppose the imperialist tactics of utilising tribalism and religious separatism to perpetuate their colonial policies in Africa'.

In resolutions such as this, both the main enemies of the nationalist élite—traditional leadership and the imperial power—have been tarred with the same evil brush. Both are accused of fomenting disunity in the colonial population. The kernel of truth in such resolutions is that imperial rule is rendered much easier by tribal and religious divisions. The irony, on the other hand, lies in the fact that just these divisions make the process of decolonisation very difficult, and in recent decades, imperial powers have been commonly found trying to pacify rather than to inflame longstanding local feuds. The British, for example, have had nothing to gain from enmities between Indian and African in Guyana, Greek and Turk in Cyprus, Chinese and Malay in Malaysia. Indeed recent colonial policy has consisted in the attempt to create federations large enough to be economically viable and capable of overriding local hostilities. This kind of policy has been tried in the Federation of the West Indies, in Aden, in Malaysia, in Nigeria, and in the complicated situation of the Rhodesias. In each case the policy has run into serious and often fatal difficulties.

What we must remember is that nowhere in the Afro-Asian world do we find a single homogeneous people dedicated to the anti-imperialist struggle. There are many occasions, perhaps most, when Buddhist and Catholic in Vietnam, Hindu and Muslim in India, Arab and Negro in the Sudan, fear each other vastly more than they hate the European power involved in their affairs. Nationalist theory and the whole conception of the anti-imperialist struggle often functions as a way of concealing a condition very close to civil war. We may, of course, find much to admire in the way in which nationalists attempt to override and divert traditional animosities; nationalism may well be interpreted as the political aspect of a struggle to divert Afro-Asian peoples away from parochial concerns towards the larger issue of modernisation. It has been created mostly by men who have spent a good deal of time living in Europe or America. If a Nigerian or an Indian, for example, spends enough time living in London or New York, he may very well come to the conclusion that the black/white struggle is far more fundamental than that between Hausa and Ibo, or between Hindu and Muslim. Further, this new struggle promises far more economically and politically than tribal or communal hatreds. It is susceptible to rational accommodation, since Britain has in the long term no vital interest in conflict with Nigeria or India. The difficulty is to sell this idea to the vast majority of natives who stay at home; and we may see nationalism throughout the Afro-Asian world as in part an attempt to do for natives who stay at home what is achieved spontaneously by those who go abroad.

Our account of Afro-Asian nationalism is broadly true of those countries which have been directly ruled by European powers in the last century or two. Even here, of course, there are many local variations. These variations are even greater where European influence has been largely indirect. We have mentioned Japan as a case where the traditional leadership managed a supremely successful modernisation without succumbing to a struggle with a nationalist élite. Another fascinating and difficult instance of non-colonial nationalism is China, which endured more than half a century of painful anarchy between the decline of her traditional regime and the arrival of a modernising government able to control the entire country. The Manchu dynasty in China was, like many other traditional rulers, in a depressed condition even in the middle of the nineteenth century; certainly it found itself unable to make any vigorous response to the challenge of Western aggressiveness. The Chinese situation was complicated by the fact that the Chinese regarded all foreigners as barbarians; and having been conquered several times by such barbarians, contempt was mixed with an element of fear. As a result, the Chinese government made an unsuccessful attempt to seal China off from foreign influences. The Opium War of 1839–42 ended this isolation with the opening to trade of five Chinese ports. From 1850 to 1864, the T'aip'ing Rebellion, whose leader characterised himself as the younger brother of Jesus and which aimed at a social revolution, gave ample warning of the possible disruptive effects of Western influence. It is said that 20 million people died in this period. China found then that she could neither ignore nor impress these new barbarians, and she was forced to find ways of coming to terms with them. As is commonly the case, the first thoughts were of taking over Western inventions like guns or steamships, and remaining just as before. But as we have observed, this cannot be done.

China had, therefore, to find new ways of conceiving of herself. And her own traditional resources gave her two modes of self-characterisation. China or the Middle Kingdom might be seen as *T'ien-hsia*, a cultural realm in which everything of value was cultivated by the mandarin class. The Chinese also had available the notion of *kuo*, a political unit conceived in terms of power. Such a unit was an area of order suppressing tendencies towards a lawless individualism. As such, it was the idea in terms of which the moral functions of the Emperor were conceived, and China herself, *T'ien-hsia*, might equally be thought of as *Chung-kuo*, the all-inclusive state, the nation. This allowed Chinese nationalists to abandon their belief in Chinese cultural superiority, and to see China in modern political terms as *kuo*, a nation free to adapt its culture according to choice.

And having abandoned the fixed China of Confucian culture, the Chinese nationalists were faced with the problem of discovering what it was that a Chinese must hold on to 'in order to maintain an independent existence on earth' (as a *Kuomintang* handbook put it in 1934).[4] A common choice was the belief that Chinese family custom constituted the essence of the nation, besides which everything else might be regarded as tactical. But the main change here was that the tradition was now coming to be thought of as something in which one might rummage for things of current value; it had never been anything like that in previous times.

Chinese nationalism was therefore a device permitting freedom of choice and the sustaining of threatened Chinese pride. And one clue to the thinking of Chinese intellectuals is the failure of Christianity. When it arrived in the country with the Portuguese in the seventeenth century, it made no impression upon a country convinced of its own superiority. After the opening up of China, Christianity might perhaps have made considerable inroads into Chinese custom as part of a reception of Western culture generally. Vast missionary effort was certainly expended in proselytising on this basis, and it had some success. The Chiang-Kai-Shek family, for example, was Methodist. Yet on the whole the effort failed, and seems to have been washed away by the Communist tide. The reason seems partly to be that many nationalist thinkers early realised that Christianity was a declining part of the Western heritage, and certainly not the part that was forcing China to change. They were therefore able to salvage Chinese pride by juxtaposing Christianity and Confucianism as Western and Eastern traditions—and rejecting both, the Western equally with the Eastern. And without prejudice to their pride, they opted in many cases for Communism as a third system which appeared untainted by the element of competition between China and the West.

The Chinese even as communists have taken an independent line, which culminated in the political split between Moscow and Peking. They based their power, against Stalin's orthodox Marxist advice,

upon the peasantry. For a long time, they did not extirpate the
previous ruling classes in the same manner and with the same
thoroughness as the Russians. In 1957, Prince Tsai T'ao, younger
brother of the Emperor Kuang Hsu who died in 1908, was not merely
living in a Communist China, but a member of the national parliament. And the mandarin class, the basis of whose power was intellectual rather than feudal, remained largely undisturbed by many
changing political fortunes. The Chinese Communist party was
founded in 1921 and managed to sustain itself through many difficult
circumstances. In 1934–5, it was forced by military defeat into the
'Long March' to the north-west, where under Mao Tse-tung it
developed the tactics of rural penetration to which it attributed its
final success in 1948. This march has become a legend in Chinese
politics; and it may equally stand as an almost irresistible allegory of
the fate of modern China—*reculer pour mieux sauter*.

This brief excursion into Chinese nationalism should illustrate the
very considerable limitations of our model, and the extremely varied
ways in which nationalist thought and feeling may operate in modern
politics. Let us now consider in rather more detail, two different
kinds of non-European nationalism; first India, which developed a
quite distinct variation of its own; and then African nationalism
which, while it has its own unique character as a doctrine, is a
representative of doctrines which are found from the bazaars of Cairo
to the rice-fields of South-East Asia.

Nationalism and Spiritual Self-Identification in India

Indian nationalism is an encounter between the mother of religions
and the mother of parliaments, and for much of the time, both were
on their best behaviour. The British came to India in the seventeenth
century, established their hegemony in the eighteenth, but consolidated direct rule of the country only in the course of the nineteenth century. One may detect a sense of awe at times in the British
attitude to the enormous country they ruled. India *was* the Empire,
an index of grandeur. She was by far the largest of the countries
governed directly by a European power; she had, also, by far the
richest civilised traditions. She had the longest direct contact with

European modes of thought. Indian nationalists early realised that the colonial destiny of India was the key to that of the rest of Asia. But their attitude to politics was complicated by an overriding moral and spiritual awareness which produced a novelty in the constellation of nationalist politics. There were times when violence was part of the story: in the terrorist wing of the Hindu extremists before 1914; in the Amritsar massacre of 1919 when General Dyer ordered his troops to fire on an Indian crowd; above all in the violent communal rioting which accompanied independence in 1947, when a large section of Muslim India split off as the state of Pakistan. This was a signal reminder that nationalism was but the last, and perhaps the most superficial, of the ways of conceiving of Indian politics. We also find, especially in later times, the sort of raucous rhetoric and superficial dogmatism about race which is a common feature of colonial and nationalist situations. But what we also find within the framework of power is a moral struggle in which each side tried to outflank the other in righteousness, the British attempting to maintain consistency with the liberal principles they professed, and the Indians led by Gandhi, the supreme tactician of this kind of struggle, attempting to exert political pressure without compromising their spiritual integrity by the use of violence. Indian nationalism is rich in variations upon this central theme.

The early Indian nationalists were not men in a hurry. Indeed, they do not appear to have had any very distinct destination. The dominating figure of this period is Dadabhai Naoraji who, in accordance with the Indian habit of giving titles, is often known as the Grand Old Man of India. He was a wealthy Parsee who spent his life trying to remedy the various injustices which he considered resulted from British rule in India. In England in 1885 he recorded in his journal for 15 April: 'Called at Dr R. Congreve's. . . . He thought the connection between England and India should be severed; it was injuring England; it was doing harm to the whole English character. The connection with the Colonies was a weakness. I was of a different opinion: that the connection should continue for the sake of India and that if certain reforms, which were sorely needed by India, were made, the connection would be a blessing to both.'[5] Addressing the second session of the Indian National Congress in 1886, he said: 'It is our good fortune that we are under a rule which makes it possible for us to meet in this manner. It is under the civilising rule of the Queen and people of England that we meet here together, hindered by none, and are freely allowed to speak our minds without the least fear and without the least hesitation. Such a thing is possible under British rule and British rule only.' These sentiments provoked cheers of approval from the assembled delegates.

By modern standards it might well be doubted whether Naoraji was a nationalist at all. He had no elaborate theory of the nation, and he did not demand independence: 'A greater calamity', he wrote, 'could not befall India than for England to go away and leave her to herself.' He simply sought for Indians the full rights of English citizenship, including participation in the government of the Empire. In 1892, he was elected to the House of Commons as Liberal member for Finsbury. His majority was three votes, and his constituents solved their difficulty in pronouncing his name by calling him Mr Narrow-Majoritee. This hard-won success in English politics did not change his criticism of imperial policy, but supplied him with an excellent platform. Among his writings is a balance-sheet of British rule in India which is a triumph of political fair-mindedness. He attempted to balance credits and debits. The British had succeeded in abolishing *suttee* and infanticide; they had destroyed the Dacoits, Thugs, Pinarees, 'and other such pests of Indian society'. Education and technology had advanced enormously, and Naoraji thought he detected 'a slowly growing desire of late to treat India equitably, and as a country held in trust. Good Intentions.' All this was on the credit side of the account. On the debit side, Naoraji considered that the *raj* involved a constant draining away of wealth from India. In modern terms, he charged that Britain was exploiting India. It was not simply the financial imbalance he deplored; it was the fact that England was failing to allow India the means by which she might pay taxation without impoverishment of capital. 'The natives call the British system *"Sakar ki Churi"*, the knife of sugar. That is to say there is no oppression, it is all smooth and sweet, but it is the knife, notwithstanding.'[6]

Naoraji is reason incarnate, a highly attractive personality whom nothing could seem to provoke into violence or self-pity. One would be unwise to expect such a tone to run through the emotions of later nationalists, whose hopes were higher and whose situation was different. Naoraji is indeed one of the founders of Nationalism, and as a 'Moderate' who supported the British connection, he was soon to be outrun by the 'Extremists' like Tilak who believed in mass support and stronger methods. But what makes Indian nationalism seem like an oasis in a desert is the fact that it never did abandon entirely some sense of the difficult balance of politics. It went through all manner of changes, and it developed, by virtue of its religious heritage, certain lines of thought which are not simply local reshufflings of the ideological elements of Western nationalism.

A more recognisably nationalist tone is to be found in Naoraji's contemporary Surendranath Banerjee, who initiated the tradition of welcoming arrest and imprisonment as a demonstration of the injustice by which he was condemned. Like the other moderates, he set great store on Hindu–Muslim co-operation. His image of a political struggle was, significantly, modelled on his knowledge of English history. He saw Indian discontents less as a national struggle than as a simple demand for liberty: 'The celestial mandate has been issued that every Indian must now do his duty, or stand condemned before God and man. There was such a time of stirring activity in the glorious annals of England, when Hampden offered up his life for the deliverance of his own country, when Algernon Sydney laid down his head on the block to rid his country of a hated tyrant, when English bishops did not hesitate in the discharge of their duty to their Fatherland to descend from the performance of their ecclesiastical functions and appear as traitors before the bar of a Criminal Court. . . . But peaceful as are the means to be enforced, there is a stern duty to be performed by every Indian. And he who fails in that duty is a traitor before God and man.'[7]

The mixture of political and moral elements commonly found in early Indian nationalism can perhaps best be typified by an extended passage from a speech made by Gopal Krishna Gokhale, the leader of the Moderates, to a conference in 1903. It takes the form of a reminiscence: 'I remember a speech delivered seven or eight years ago by the late Mr Ranade in Bombay, under the auspices of the Hindu Union Club. That was a time when public feeling ran high in

India on the subject of the treatment which our people were receiving in South Africa. Our friend, Mr Gandhi, had come here on a brief visit from South Africa and he was telling us how our people were treated in Natal and Cape Colony and the Transvaal—how they were not allowed to walk on footpaths or travel in first-class carriages on the railway, how they were not admitted into hotels, and so forth. Public feeling, in consequence, was deeply stirred. . . . But it was Mr Ranade's peculiar greatness that he always utilised occasions of excitement to give a proper turn to the national mind and cultivate its sense of proportion. And so, when everyone was expressing himself in indignant terms about the treatment which our countrymen were receiving in South Africa, Mr Ranade came forward to ask if we had no sins of our own to answer for in that direction. I do not exactly remember the title of his address. I think it was "Turn the searchlight inwards", or some such thing. But I remember that it was a great speech—one of the greatest I have ever been privileged to hear. He began in characteristic fashion, expressing deep sympathy with the Indians in South Africa in the struggle they were manfully carrying on. He rejoiced that the people of India had awakened to a sense of the position of their countrymen abroad, and he felt convinced that this awakening was a sign of the fact that the dead bones in the valley were once again becoming instinct with life. But he proceeded to ask: "Was this sympathy with the oppressed and downtrodden Indians to be confined to those of our countrymen only who had gone out of India? Or was it to be general and to be extended to all cases where there was oppression and injustice?" It was easy, he said, to denounce foreigners, but those who did so were bound in common fairness to look into themselves and see if they were not absolutely blameless in the matter. He then described the manner in which members of low caste were treated by their own community in different parts of India. It was a description which filled the audience with feelings of deep shame and pain and indignation. . . .'[8]

Perhaps it is true that the display of so exquisite a spirit of self-examination in politics is a luxury available only to the contentedly powerless. The early members of Congress were a tiny minority of well-to-do Indians who had enjoyed—as the excellent English in which they wrote testifies—a sound Western education. Their situation resembled that of the German nationalists: they were isolated between the generally indifferent British administration and the masses of ordinary Indians to whom their preoccupations were as nothing. They did not have the option of ruling India on equal terms with the British; and any attempt to rouse the masses was, for such respectable men, the equivalent of unbottling a peculiarly malicious and unpredictable *djinn*. Nonetheless, as Indian confidence steadily increased, so larger numbers of Indians were likely to be drawn into a national struggle whose outcome was unpredictable. The first stages of this new development came early in the new century under the leadership of Bal Gangadhar Tilak.

Tilak sounded a more familiar nationalist note. He fought the Moderates with such slogans as 'Militancy—not mendicancy'. This is an early use of what was later to become a prominent feature of modern nationalism—its appeal to dignity, which begging would prejudice. Fundamentally, Tilak's problem was that Indians, high and low, tended to regard the Englishman as belonging to a higher order of things. Politically they lacked a sense of their own strength. 'Every Englishman', Tilak told them, 'knows that they are a mere handful in this country and it is the business of every one of them to befool you in believing that you are weak and they are strong. This is politics.' From 1905 onwards, Indian confidence was steadily increasing. A sense that Britain was not the only giant in the European world began to affect Congress leaders, and Congress itself was coming to count for more. The Russo–Japanese War of 1904–5 was important to all Asian nationalist feeling. Europeans had been defeated in war by an Asian power. In Curzon's famous remark, 'The reverberations of that victory have gone like a thunderclap through the whispering galleries of the East.' In 1907 Congress split between the Moderates led by G. K. Gokhale and the Extremists led by Tilak. Tilak accepted the use of these terms, but put his own gloss upon them: 'The Extremists of today will be Moderates tomorrow, just as the Moderates of today were Extremists yesterday . . . the term Extremist is an expression of progress.' From 1907 to 1912 there were sporadic outbreaks of terrorist violence, to which Tilak's attitude was ambiguous. He was consequently sent to prison in 1908, but this did not put an end to the violence. Terror was clearly one option open to the Indian nationalist movement; and so blunt an instrument might well in India have had appalling consequences. Its avoidance was due largely to the character of the men who successively dominated Congress.

Tilak was the sort of nationalist whom any European would recognise as such. He came from a Brahmin background, but he was prepared to appeal to the masses of India in a way which made his Moderate colleagues in Congress fear that he was jeopardising Indian constitutional evolution towards self-government within the Empire. In effect, Tilak faced the problem of identifying, indeed of inventing, an Indian nation. For such an identification, he needed a glorious past in which Indians could take pride. The problem here was not that India lacked a glorious past, but that she had too many of them, and each was involved with communal animosities in the present. Tilak was an aggressive Hindu patriot. Distinguished also as a theologian, he re-stated the message of the *Bhagavad Gita* as a call to political action in the world. That one must perform one's social duties is indeed the explicit message of the Lord Krishna in the *Chita*, but Tilak harnessed the usages of Hinduism to the nationalist struggle. He established a society to prevent the killing of cows, a point of religious orthodoxy which owes its present high status to the nationalist enthusiasm of that time. And he made a hero out of Shivagji, a seventeenth-century Maratha chieftain who had harassed the Mogul emperors who ruled before the British.

These tactics were unpalatable to the Muslims, who made up about a quarter of the population. The Muslims were the rock on which most of the hopeful assertions of Indian nationalism were to founder. As Muhammid Ali remarked in 1912, the Muslim community had 'lagged behind in the race by moodily sulking in its tents and declining, for a considerable time, to avail itself of the facilities for intellectual and material progress'.[9] The Muslims were not prepared to allow religious and racial differences in India to be regarded as merely private concerns subordinate to a public attachment to the Indian nation. And the democratic sentiments of Congress leaders meant for most Muslims only the certainty of being ruled by a hostile Hindu majority. As Sir Syed Ahmad Khan (1817–98) put it: 'I studied John Stuart Mill's views in support of representative government. He has dealt with this matter exceedingly well in great detail. I reached the conclusion that the first requisite of a representative government is that the voters should possess the highest degree of homogeneity. . . . The aims and objects of the Indian National Congress are based upon an ignorance of history and present-day realities; they do not take into consideration that India is inhabited by different nationalities.'

The dilemma facing Indian nationalists was perfectly clear: unless they appealed to religion, then nationalism would be limited to the small educated élite, and consequently more or less powerless. If, however, they appealed to the tremendous resources of Hindu spirituality, then they were going to destroy the unity of India.

One of Tilak's lieutenants in the period up to 1910 was the mystic and philosopher Sri Aurobindo Ghosh. His involvement with the nationalist movement was short but intense, and it illustrates both the similarities between Indian nationalist thought and its European models, and also the particular twist given to this model by Indian mystical concerns. Aurobindo takes India commonly to be a mother to whom duties are owed by her faithful sons. 'Love has a place in politics, but it is love of one's country, for one's countrymen, for the glory, greatness and happiness of the race, the divine *ananda* of self-immolation for one's fellows, the ecstasy of relieving their sufferings, the joy of seeing one's blood flow for country and freedom, the bliss of union in death with the fathers of the race. The feeling of almost physical delight in the touch of the mother-soil, of the winds that blow from Indian seas, of the rivers that stream from Indian hills, in the hearing of Indian speech, music, poetry, in the familiar sights, sounds, habits, dress, manners of our Indian life, this is the physical root of that love. The pride in our past, the pain of our present, the passion for the future are its trunk and branches. Self-sacrifice and self-forgetfulness, great service, high endurance for country are its point. And the sap which keeps it alive is the realisation of the Motherhood of God in the country, the perpetual contemplation, adoration and service of the Mother.'[10]

This passage is in many ways a typical example of the newspaper rhetoric of Indian nationalism. It is characterised by a poetic fluency which seems to come easily to Indian writers, and which is dangerously close to an almost complete vacuity of meaning. In Aurobindo, a guiding thread is visible, and the thread is clearly religious. 'There are times in a nation's history when Providence places before it one work, one aim, to which everything else, however high and noble in itself, has to be sacrificed.' The language of ethical idealism, with its Hindu passion for sacrifice conceived as the surrender of individuality, leads to the kind of remark which has often been used to cloak violence and terror: 'Nationalism is not a mere political programme; nationalism is a religion that has come from God. You must remember that you are an instrument of God.' But our fears that this Mazzinian language might presage some kind of Machiavellian *raison de nation*, defending any enormity if it free the nation, are unfounded in the case of Aurobindo. Others at this time did begin to learn how to make and throw bombs; but in Aurobindo's case, religious and mystical convictions had been but lightly touched by nationalist influences. He very soon abandoned active politics. He was clearing his mind for divine inspiration, and the message which he claimed to have come to him in prison was a kind of Hindu pantheism. Divinity is in everything, in what opposes as in what supports nationalism. And India's national purpose is to be a spiritual guide to the world.

Superficially this looks like a religious version of the doctrine of national mission. What in fact has happened is that Aurobindo has gone straight past nationalism into something which it would be crude even to describe as religious internationalism. In Aurobindo's case the Hindu religion is not a nationally identifying instrument of nationalism. On the contrary, the political has been subordinated to the religious. Aurobindo here exhibits in an acute form a common ambiguity of Indian nationalism. The straightforward Westernised nationalists, of whom Pandit Nehru was a pre-eminent and complicated example, were greatly outnumbered by those whose nationalism was but one strand of thought and action. Only by calling upon India's spiritual enthusiasm could Indian nationalism become a powerful mass movement; but in doing so, politics ran the serious danger of being swamped by religion. In principle, there is no solution for a dilemma of this kind. Reality, however, supplied one kind of solution in the person of Mahatma Gandhi.

Gandhi was the culmination of that process by which Indian

nationalism spread out from its base in the tiny Westernised middle class and became a mass movement agitating the passions of the Indian masses, right down to the village level. Tilak and the Extremists had started this process with their Hindu revivalism and their demand for *Swaraj* or self-rule. Between 1916 and 1920 Gandhi took over control of Congress and gained almost unanimous support for his policy of non-violent resistance. He was by this time a mature man of nearly 50 with a history of successful communal agitation behind him in South Africa. He had prepared himself for the inevitable rigours of the policy he suggested by taking a vow of chastity (he was married and had had several children) and practising an austere and simple form of life. He was a vegetarian, and he abandoned Western modes of dress. These practices not only steeled his spirit; they gave him certain unassailable political advantages in India. He was a man of the people by virtue of his comparatively humble origins (he was of the *vaishya* caste) and simple mode of life; more than that, he had the look of a saint. He combined sanctity and political acumen uniquely. Only such a man could have prevented the fissiparous elements of Indian politics from exploding into violence during the period from 1920 to 1947.

His nationalism was of Western origins. He took all India to be a political unit which ought to be democratic. He included in this India both the Untouchables and the Muslims, and his finally unsuccessful attempt to include Muslim India in the nationalist movement also cost him his life. A Hindu fanatic shot him in 1948. Certain of his notions of pacificism could be backed by the views of Tolstoy or Kropotkin. And his English legal training was indispensable in guiding the policy of the Congress. Yet it is difficult not to feel that these Western influences were but superficial, and that everything Gandhi absorbed was transmuted by his Hindu syncretism. This Hindu element appeared certainly in many superficial details of his mode of life as a public figure—in his dress, his food, his fasts, his manner of dealing with people. On the other hand, he was a Hindu saint in a novel, Western type of situation. He himself commented on the combination of saint and politician within him; and concluded that he was a politician trying to be a saint. But then, that itself, by its humility, would be the saintly self-characterisation. What we must recognise is that both saint and politician were parts of his personality, neither entirely subordinate to the other. But such formulae leave us a long way from understanding the man himself.

And it is the man who must be understood, for the ideas were not universally accepted in his lifetime, and have weakened in influence since then. The Westernised middle class accepted Gandhi with reservations, or perhaps out of atavistic respect for his conspicuous sanctity. Most nationalists found it hard to follow his systematic rejection of all the economic elements of modernisation. Gandhi disliked the mechanised aspects of the modern world. 'My Hinduism', he wrote, 'is not sectarian. It includes all that I know to be best in Islam, Christianity, Buddhism, and Zoroastrianism. I approach politics as everything else in a religious spirit. Truth is my religion and *ahimsa* [non-violence] is the only way of its realisation.'[11] He attacked a civilisation which made people's bodily welfare the object of life. 'Formerly, only a few men wrote valuable books. Now, anybody writes and prints anything he likes and poisons people's minds. . . . Formerly when people wanted to fight with one another, they measured between them their bodily strength; now it is possible to take away thousands of lives by one man working behind a gun from a hill.'[12] There is a certain machine-gun quality about this kind of rhetoric—everything is sprayed with paper bullets. But its force in Indian nationalism comes not in passages of this kind, but in the related cult of the spinning wheel and the encouragement of traditional Indian cottage industry. Gandhi considered that modern industry would change the Indian character; and unlike most nationalists who recognise this, he was prepared to sacrifice material prosperity to the maintenance of spiritual integrity.

This is the central principle, too, of the doctrine of *satyagraha*, which is the power exerted by a truthful soul. It was Gandhi's substitute for violence in bringing the British to recognise the rights and the strength of Indians. Politically, it was a brilliant solution to the problems of Congress. It was activist and it involved large numbers of people; at one stage 34,000 were in prison. On the other hand, it avoided violence, with its incalculable consequences. It put the British morally on the defensive, and denied them the righteousness of suppressing a threat to law and order. Gandhi denied that it was simply a weapon of the weak. 'Everybody admits that sacrifice of self is infinitely superior to sacrifice of others. Moreover, if this kind of force is used in a cause that is unjust, only the person using it suffers. He does not make others suffer for his mistakes.'[13]

We have seen, in countries as diverse as India and Germany, a similar pattern arise within nationalist movements. There are those who seek to follow the liberal West, and those who feel that it threatens national distinctiveness; the Westernisers and (to use the Russian terminology) the Slavophils. Gandhi belonged distinctly to the second group of nationalists. It was his tactics and largely his ideas which dominated the period up to the partition of India. An independent India has had a number of second thoughts; patriotic inflammation over war with China and Pakistan generated in India a noticeable impatience with non-violence. But even in Gandhi's own period, there were many who saw his influence as partly retrogressive. The most interesting of these is the towering figure of Rabindranath Tagore, whose first reaction to Gandhi was one of great enthusiasm. 'We, the famished ragged ragamuffins of the East', he wrote in a letter in 1921, 'are to win freedom for all humanity.'[14] He agreed with Gandhi in hating many things that he found in the West, and expressed his feelings in that Indian manner of which he was supremely a master. 'I have seen the West; I covet not the unholy feast in which she revels every moment, growing more and more bloated and red and dangerously delirious. Not for us is this mad orgy of midnight, with lighted torches, but awakenment in the serene light of the morning.'[15]

Yet Tagore, though a national figure, strongly opposed nationalism. His image of nationalism came from the clash of European powers in the war of 1914. He pointed out that Indians had no word for 'nation' and that even when borrowed it sat ill upon their character. But even more, he opposed nationalism wherever he found it on the grounds that it cramped the human spirit. 'When nature called to the bee to take refuge in the narrow life of the hive, millions of bees responded to it for the sake of efficiency, and accepted the loss of sex in consequence. But this sacrifice by way of self-atrophy led to the opposite of freedom. Any country, the people of which can agree to become neuters for the sake of some temptation, or command, carries within itself its own prison-house.'[16] This is a liberal and humanist position difficult to reconcile with the details of any nationalist movement. Tagore could see no virtue in 'going backwards'. Gandhi, by contrast, wrote: 'India's salvation consists in unlearning what she has learned during the last fifty years. The railways, telegraphs, hospitals, lawyers, doctors and suchlike have all to go; and the so-called upper classes have to learn consciously, religiously, and deliberately the simple peasant life.'[17] Gandhi's non-cooperation movement in 1921 consequently branched out into a full-scale attack upon Western influences, and culminated in the burning of foreign cloth in huge flaming pyramids which silhouetted passionate nationalists addressing crowds of up to 160,000 people. Self-rule, or *swaraj*, was to be an economic as well as a political matter.

In opposing this movement, Tagore represents one further refraction of Indian nationalism. He considered that Gandhi's notion of *swaraj* was materialist, and that genuine self-rule came only with the dignity of self-reliance and self-mastery in the spiritual world, to 'those whom no temptation, no delusion, can induce to surrender the dignity of intellect into the keeping of others. . . . Where Mahatma Gandhi', he went on, 'has declared war against the tyranny of the machine which is oppressing the whole world, we are all enrolled under his banner. But we must refuse to accept as our ally the illusion-haunted, magic-ridden, slave-mentality that is at the root of all the poverty and insult under which our country groans. Here is the enemy itself, on whose defeat alone *swaraj* within and without can come to us.'[18]

We have suggested that nationalism is a collective grievance against a foreign oppressor. India had a foreign oppressor in the form of the British *raj*. We have, in the flood of Indian nationalist writings, done no more than take a bucket from Niagara. But this is perhaps enough to show the way in which some Indian writers managed to explore the ambiguities of the relationship between oppressor and oppressed, and how some even began to generalise the grievance and find new locations for it. 'In some part or other of every nation', Tagore wrote, 'some lurking greed or illusion still perpetuates bondage. And the root of such bondage is always within the mind. Where then, I ask again, is the argument, that in our country *swaraj* can be brought about by everyone engaging for a time in spinning?'[19] The intellectual interest of such writings is that they press nationalist rhetoric to its limits, and then, undisturbed by immediate political considerations, keep reasoning onwards.

African Nationalism

In the African beginning was the tribe. It might be a small nomadic group of closely related people whose political structure was so negligible as to cause anthropologists to coin the word 'acephalous', lacking a head or chief. It might alternatively be a dispersed and populous group like the Bantu, the Buganda or the Hausa, all of which have many of the characteristics of nations. And like nations, most tribes have a history of animosities which have caused enduring fear and rivalry between them. The modern African state was a new dimension superimposed upon the tribes in the European 'scramble for Africa' in the 1880s. The boundaries of such states often cut straight across those of the tribe, so that parts of the same tribe may encounter modernity in a French, or a British, or a Portuguese form. These modern states are artificial constructions, but in the last 50 to 100 years they have become the basis of literacy, transport and bureaucracy in Africa, and they cannot be lightly discarded. It was to these states that independence came in the period between 1955 and 1965. Independence brought with it a set of politicians and administrators whose power and prosperity largely depend upon keeping things as they are. But each of these politicians is impelled onwards to yet a third element of African politics: Africa itself. Pan-Africanism looks forward to the federation or union of all Africans under one government which would exert a strong influence on the destiny of the world.

But what would be federated? The geographical continent of Africa is inhabited not only by a preponderance of black Africans, but also in the north by the Arabs of Egypt and the Maghrib, and in the south by a small but militarily formidable set of whites. Although Africans and Arabs might well in a nationalist mood feel like brothers conducting a struggle against imperialism, no one seriously believes that they could unite in a single viable state. The Arabs hearken to the call of Islam, while black Africa develops the concept of 'negritude'; meanwhile 'Africa' remains a slightly hazy concept compounded of a continent and a colour.

The tribe continues to be the focus of loyalty for the majority of Africans. The reason for this is that most Africans have very little intimate and direct contact with Europeans, whilst they have many very direct contacts with other Africans. A somewhat crude confirmation of this is the fact that Africans killed far more Africans than Europeans in the turbulent post-war struggles. An estimated 3,000 Africans were casualties in the Mau Mau uprisings in Kenya; Europeans and Asians killed numbered 58.[20] Violence against whites in Nigeria has been virtually unknown in recent times; but intertribal struggles have taken a considerable toll.

It may at first seem strange that nationalism flies directly in the face of tribal realities in Africa, and concerns itself with the comparatively remote imperial power: but herein lies its central endeavour. It consists in the attempt to replace existing animosities with a new and different kind of struggle. Tribal animosity, if it benefits anyone at all, benefits the traditional rulers, the very people whom nationalist politicians seek to render impotent and replace. Further, tribal strife is a serious drag upon the progress of African states in coming to terms with modern life.

There is another reason why African nationalism is so extensively concerned with black and white relations. This is that it was first developed by the Africans of what are commonly called, by analogy with Jewish experience, the diaspora. Just as the Jews under the Roman Empire were driven from their homeland and scattered over the face of Europe and Asia in the dispersion, so also were thousands of Africans forcibly removed from their tribes and forced into slavery in the New World. The slave trade abolished only in the nineteenth century created millions of detribalised Africans living in the Americas. These were the Africans who first began to question their identity in relation to white civilisation. They were attracted by the idea of an African homeland where they might settle away from the white man, but of many projects, only Liberia came to fruition. The men who promoted pan-African ideas were educated, and education had an entirely Western content. Western education almost inevitably involves an irrational element of group pride in belonging to the same people as Shakespeare, or Pasteur, or Luther, or Galileo. Africans must largely find that the content of education is the achievement of a foreign people. They might identify themselves with Hannibal in his struggle with Rome, seeing in this an analogue of Africa's struggle with the West. Or they might take pride in ancient Egyptian civilisation, located in Africa and arguably the work of a negroid people.[21] For the most part the primitivism of African conditions was a standing contrast to all that a Western education taught them to admire. In this situation, romantic and nationalist doctrines have had an irresistible appeal because, given that Africans choose to see themselves as a group (and many hostile circumstances in the world encourage such a vision), then the one initial characteristic of which they cannot be deprived is their uniqueness. The problem then becomes one of discovering elements of value in this uniqueness. The achievements of negroes in music and art allow of a general attribution of spontaneity to negroes such as is lacking in the materialistic and calculating West. A theory of 'negritude' such as the French-trained particularly have extracted from this situation can therefore function not only as a defensive weapon against Western presumptions; it can also turn into an aggressive weapon pointing to defects in Western civilisation itself.

Given the situation of the black Africans, it is hardly surprising that some notions of negritude should have led to excesses. The findings of African history and archaeology have been watched with a nervous *political* anxiety for signs of grandeur in the African past. Again, philosophy is concerned with highly general questions which cannot be subordinated to political requirements; its character is therefore misconceived when the African philosopher, 'faced by the totalitarian or egocentric philosophers of the West', is called upon by the Conference of Negro Writers and Artists, meeting in Rome in 1959, 'to divest himself of a possible inferiority complex, which might prevent him from starting from his African *being* [their italics] to judge the foreign contribution'.[22] The same kind of preoccupation is to be found in the All-African Peoples' Conference held in Cairo in 1961 demanding 'the reorganisation of Education in such a way as to remove from curricula all ideas tending to give the African a sense of inferiority, and to re-establish authentic history'. Nothing in education *logically* involves anyone in a feeling of inferiority (however *natural* such inferences may be thought) and any attempt to falsify knowledge so as to boost African confidence is itself an implicit admission of inferiority. These attitudes, we may repeat, are understandable excesses arising from a social situation; what is perhaps less to be expected is the robust scepticism of many African writers and artists themselves about any special claims to a specifically African kind of uniqueness. Such a scepticism is a sign, not of nationalism with its emphasis upon group identification, but of individualism which cuts the knot of group inferiority exactly at its source.

The development of African nationalism took place primarily in Europe. Congresses were held in a number of European cities; only after 1958 did it return to its purported homeland. Those who developed nationalist doctrines were at first American and West Indian negroes, who had experience of intimate and direct contact with whites, and consequently with racial discrimination. Soon they were joined, and eventually swamped, by indigenous African intellectuals, students who resided often for many years in London and Paris, and there, after the manner of nationalist exiles, had begun to rethink the situation of Africa.

It was in London, for example, that Kwame Nkrumah worked for the independence of Ghana and of West Africa generally. He spent twelve years abroad, in the United States and Great Britain. In London he formed a nationalist organisation called 'The Circle', a body clearly descended from the secret societies of Young Italy, the cells of Russian revolutionaries and, above all, from the Leninist organisation of Communists before 1917. The Circle was dedicated to 'Service, Sacrifice, Suffering'. It aimed 'to maintain ourselves and the Circle as the Revolutionary Vanguard of the struggle for West African Unity and National Independence'. With perhaps a reminiscence of Gandhian ideas, members of the Circle were enjoined on the 21st day of the month to fast from sunrise to sunset, and to meditate daily on the cause the Circle stood for. And it made a case for its necessity by an abstract characterisation of its enemies: it sought to make it 'impossible and difficult for demagogues, quislings, traitors, cowards and self-seekers to lead astray any section of the masses of the African peoples'.[23] These phrases contain some typical features of nationalist political discourse. Before discussing these features, let us consider one or two more examples. The independent African states soon split into two groups, the Monrovia group which Western observers considered 'moderate', and the Casablanca Six which was similarly regarded as 'extremist'. Ghana belonged to the Casablanca Six and, in 1962, when the Monrovia powers were meeting at Lagos, a Ghanaian paper characterised the two groups as follows: 'Economically, the Casablanca Six have established their economic independence and are exploiting their national wealth for the benefit of their masses while the members of the French Community as well as many of the former British colonies continue to be exploited by their former colonialist masters. Their people still toil in poverty while Europe saps their wealth.'[24] Or, again, in a maze of resolutions all couched in the same language, we might pick at random: 'The Third All-African Peoples' Conference notes with satisfaction the intensification of the struggle of the African peoples for the achievement of their political independence with a view to decolonising the political, economic and social structures of Africa.'[25]

In all these examples, we must immediately observe how abstract and intellectual is the language of discourse. It is far more intellectual than the kind of language we find being used by, say, British or American politicians. The question arises, then, why do we find highly abstract language being directed at people whom we must assume in view of their lack of political experience to be politically unsophisticated? Terms like 'exploitation', 'colonialism', 'reactionary forces', 'opportunist elements', etc., stand for vague and complicated ideas which can only with great difficulty, if at all, be understood in terms of the everyday reality of an African (or anyone else, for that matter). This is true even of statements which appear to recognise this very difficulty—as when it is said, for example, that the Westminster model of democracy is 'out of touch with African realities'. The key to African nationalism would seem to lie in understanding the oddity of its complicated rhetoric. And we may suggest a number of partial solutions. In the first place, we may observe that the intellectual content of these terms is largely irrelevant; and it is implicitly recognised as such in the inevitable switching of political alliances which mean that a politician characterised as 'reactionary' at one moment becomes 'progressive' the next. For given a free-association test, the simplest African political worker will give the right evaluative replies: 'exploitation—bad', 'democratic instrument —good', 'colonialism—bad', and so on. This is a rhetorical language of highly intellectual and abstract words being used for exceptionally simple emotional purposes. It hardly takes either courage or perception to attack 'demagogues, quislings, traitors, cowards and self-seekers'; this is a clergyman declaring himself against sin to an audience of lay preachers.

Next we may observe that this is a language full of technical jargon, and like all technical terminology, it impresses people—and is often deliberately cultivated because it does so. African nationalism rests upon a highly explicit rejection of anything like Plato's philosopher kings—a role more likely to be claimed by the European district officer. As Nkrumah put it: 'It is far better to be free to govern, or misgovern yourself than to be governed by anyone else.'[26] Nevertheless, African nationalist politicians implicitly claim a right to rule on the basis of a technical skill; they claim to understand the intercontinental threats of European imperialists to the African people.

So far we have not considered the content of African nationalist discourse. What is its political theory? We find on examination that it consists of three elements, nationalist, liberal and Leninist. The first is a familiar nationalist element used for identifying, claiming a mission for, and guiding, the African people. There is a claim to uniqueness, to a destiny in the world. And here nationalists use a common device of those who need a glorious past but have difficulty in discovering one: they transfer their allegiance to a glorious future. They claim that Africa is a new nation which will take up the torch of a barren and impoverished European culture.

The second element is one which was also prominent in Indian thought—a liberal democratic strand. An allegiance to democracy is virtually universal in the twentieth century; in Africa it makes good political sense because Africans are in a majority in their states. The application of democratic procedures is thus an immediate arrival of nationalist politicians to power. This liberal strand also contains appeals to justice and human rights, which are considered at a discount in a colonial situation. The crown of this strand of thought is the demand for freedom—whether it be spelt as *Uhuru*, or *liberté*.

Lastly, African nationalism is partly composed of African socialism, an eclectic form of Marxism. Vulgar Marxism, and at times Marx himself, had upheld the idea of a class whose essential characteristic was that it was victimised; this class was, of course, the proletariat. The kind of victimisation it endured was called exploitation, a form of robbery by which it received less than it had produced. African nationalists have at times taken the African peoples as an essentially victimised race. In addition, the Marxist philosophy of history has been adapted to African uses. The bad past was a time of traditional and imperialist rule, whilst the inevitable and good future was evolution towards a united, rich and powerful Africa, under nationalist rule. This philosophy could be used against tribal leaders, who were not only bad but also doomed. What supported tradition could then be dubbed 'reactionary'—a concept which mixes the deplorable with the doomed—whilst nationalist leadership stood for progress.

The Marxist content of African socialism is, however, deceptive, for the style of function of this strand of thought is actually Leninist. Leninism is a political language appropriate to a political vanguard which knows what it must do, but finds itself ruling a population with quite other ideas. It is an authoritarian theory which must appear somehow democratic. It conceives of politics in terms of élites and masses, and operates as an instrument by which the leadership or vanguard may impose its will upon the masses. The use of technical jargon of a somewhat empty kind is a useful part of this process. It simultaneously baffles the mind and guides the feet.

Conceived as a philosophy of politics, African socialism has nothing which need detain the academic tourist. But the point of such ideologies is not to be intellectually coherent but to fit into a political programme. African nationalists are seeking, among other things, to Westernise their countries. They do not wish to become a troubled sea in which outside powers may seek advantages—this is the fear of 'Balkanisation' which crops up increasingly in African politics. The assumption that Africa is a homogeneous unit helps to keep that particular fear at bay. One student of African politics, Colin Legum, quotes with approval the Kenyan politician Tom Mboya saying: 'We find that both Westerners and Russians look at Africans through the same pair of glasses: the one lens is marked pro-West; the other pro-Communist. It is not surprising that, looking at Africans in this way, most foreigners fail to understand the one great reality about our continent—that Africans are neither pro-West nor pro-Russian; they are pro-African.'[27] But this is to beg the question: no one is agreed what it is, in fluid political situations, to be 'pro-African', and both communist and Western states have an interest in the conceptions of it that may arise. The game is really given away by the fact that one of the great tactical categories of nationalist in-fighting is that of 'stooge', which is precisely the charge that some African politicians are being pro-something else than Africa.

With these considerations in view, we may return to the question we raised at the beginning of this chapter: Is nationalism, in the words of the newspaper cliché, the strongest political force in the modern world? We noted then that a hostile characterisation would be that African nationalism is the work of a few agitators. To take the hostile characterisation first, we may agree that African nationalism is in part the work of an ambitious class of African politicians who have displayed considerable energy, and also great talent, in changing African politics. Like all politicians, they are disposed to quarrel among themselves, and it is possible that their internal struggles will defeat their nationalist aims. But those who claim to stand for 'civilisation' have also their own interests to defend—generally the interests of white settlers in the southern part of Africa. We must avoid one of the great errors of political discussion—accepting a characterisation of one party in terms of abstract principle (reason, civilisation, right-thinking) and of another party in terms of its interests (ambition, self-seeking). On both sides, we shall always find both interests and principles.

As a 'force in the modern world' African nationalist leaders may be seen as men who have been trying to divert the energy of Africans away from tribal animosity into the different channel of hating and fighting 'imperialists'—a political category partly real and partly imaginary. In this endeavour, in the two decades following the end of the war in 1945, they seemed to have had great success. But it was in part an easy success: in most areas, the imperial powers were little disposed to resist. Nationalists were also fairly successful in defeating competition from the traditional leadership of Africa. On the eve of independence, every nationalist leader has warned that the struggle is just beginning. But which struggle? Many Africans had acquired, as a debris of nationalist enthusiasm, the belief that independence was the solution to all problems. It has rather been, as Brian Crozier puts it, a 'morning after' a long intoxication.[28] The most difficult struggle waged by the African leaders is no doubt to modernise their countries, a struggle lacking in the glamour of politics. When this proves too difficult, the politician in what we have called the consolidation period may well be tempted into the melodrama of shadow boxing: 'The situation demands our constant watchfulness and vigilance. All imperialist intrigues, manoeuvres and acts of subversion aimed at discrediting the independent African States and undermining their tranquillity and security must be unmasked and exposed as part of a consorted [*sic*] plan by the colonialist powers to keep Africa divided and weak.'[29] This is to make of independence merely the continuation of political excitement by other means; and it directs energy away from the real source of African weakness. It is here that we may see a theme that tends to repeat itself in the history of nationalism: success tends to corrupt, and politics is a vehicle of fantasy. The fate dreaded by intelligent Africans is the disorder of the Balkans and the stagnation of nineteenth-century Latin America. So far, African nationalism has been an instrument for engaging more and more Africans in the task of modernising their continent. But there are some features of African nationalist thought which, although useful in the period of nationalist struggle, are positively retrogressive in the period of national consolidation. But history cannot be caught on the wing, and this particular bird is still very much in flight.

5

The Equipment of
a Proper Nation

National Symbols

New nations, nowadays, begin at midnight with a ceremony in which
the imperial flag is lowered and the new national anthem sung as the
new flag unfurls. The flag must become to the nation what colours
are to a regiment—a focus for emotion and a guide in moments of
confusion. Flags and anthems can be used to create members of a
nation by developing new habits and emotions; the Star Spangled
Banner with its stars increasing as new states joined the Union was
an important symbol of America to the millions of immigrants to the
United States. This process takes time, and flags generally survive
most political upheavals in national politics. There have been
occasions, however, when a new regime, intent upon signalising in
every possible way the novelty of the revolution, has changed the
flag. In this way, the *Tricolore* became the French flag, and the
Hammer and Sickle the Russian. In these cases, the release of new
enthusiasm must replace the habits of reverence developed over a
long period. Most nationalist politicians hope that the attainment of
independence will generate this kind of enthusiasm.

National anthems require great care. They may often enshrine
irrelevant emotions—the Dutch have a national anthem referring
back to their struggles against Philip II of Spain, whilst the *Marseillaise*, perhaps the most stirring of all national anthems, is a bloodthirsty call to arms encouraging the children of the *patrie* to water the
furrows of France with the blood of the enemy. Such anthems recall
times of enthusiasm which are saved from absurdity only by their
place in a heroic past. Generally, it is a serious mistake to embody

passing enthusiasms in the words of an anthem: Bulgaria has been stuck for some time with an anthem about 'the great sun of Lenin and Stalin which lit our way with its rays', whilst Ghana's anthem praised Nkrumah the Redeemer. Nationalist theory requires that a national anthem should 'express the deepest aspirations of the nation'; and this often means that the words carry a heavy ideological cargo. Perhaps the safest way of connecting the national anthem with the national soul is to give an old tune new words—and to ban the original version.

We have already noted that rivers, mountain ranges and the sea are regarded in nationalist thought as divine hints about frontiers—usually expansive, it should be added, for there are no cases of nations actually abandoning territory in order to achieve such a rational scheme. Still, this view is one rationalist element in nationalist thought, one point where the historical bias of nationalism is abandoned in favour of an abstract geography. Thus the early nineteenth-century nationalist Friedrich Jahn suggested that a united Germany should have a new capital called Teutonia built in the centre of the country.[1] The creation of Brasilia in the vast hinterland of Brazil is a deliberately rational project of a similar sort. It was designed to induce Brazilians to abandon such crowded coastal locations as Rio de Janeiro and develop the national resources of the interior. India was already equipped by the British with a refurbished capital in Delhi. The Turkish nation moved its capital from cosmopolitan Istanbul on the Bosphorus, to Ankara. The weight of thought behind these changes seems to be a conception of the nation as a solid lump of territory, inhabited by a homogeneous people, and visualised as a circle. The frontiers are the circumference of this circle, and the capital should be its centre, for in this way is minimised the distance between the capital and any of the provinces. Historically, capital cities have often developed either from dynastic pressures or because of considerations of economic geography now irrelevant. New nations like to build new ones. Failing a new capital, then the existing capital should be equipped with new prestige buildings: government buildings are essential, followed soon in those nations which can afford it with a sports stadium and international conference centre, buildings which give to nationals the same sense of solid worth as an opera-house used to give to the citizens of the cowboy towns of the Wild West.

If the nation is too poor for the moment to build such glittering new symbols of nationhood, a similar effect can be achieved at less cost by changing of names. The names of most colonial territories were heavy with traces of the colonial past—a weight symbolised by the number of statues of Queen Victoria with which the British Empire chose to litter the continents of the world. They were soon torn down as one of the first rewards of freedom and as a declaration of aesthetic independence. In Africa, the actual name of the nation has often been invented from scratch. The Gold Coast Colony chose, on independence, to become Ghana, thus attaching itself to the traditions of a medieval empire of which little was known, except that it did not include the Gold Coast area. Pakistan was a nation defying almost all the criteria of nationhood except that of religious homogeneity. It consists of two almost equally populous lumps of territory on the northern borders of India. Its name was invented by a Cambridge undergraduate in 1930, and was constructed from the initials of Muslim provinces of India to mean 'land of the pure'. And just as the names of states may be changed on the attainment of independence, so also may the names of cities and of streets. Names like Rhodes, Albert, Leopold and Victoria are likely to give way to indigenous creations, and the heroes of independence are commemorated in the names of streets. The capital of the Congo, once Leopoldville, has turned into Kinshasa. Occasionally quite subtle games can be played in this way. Chinese extremists in Peking in 1966 renamed the street where the Russian Embassy stands 'the street of the struggle against revisionism'.

There was a time before nationalism when a religion was thought to be an essential piece of equipment for any nation-state. This had ceased to be obligatory before nationalist thought developed. Many countries, however, remain so overwhelmingly devoted to one religion that it may suitably be considered as part of the essence of the nation. In the case of the Republic of Ireland, allegiance to Catholicism is explicitly stated in the constitution, and Catholicism is a central tradition of countries like Spain, Portugal and Italy. Islamic republics go so far as to reject the common Western distinction between public citizenship and private religious belief. This is one ground of dispute between India, which is a secular republic, and Pakistan, whose nationhood is defined in terms of Islam.

The exigencies of modern political struggles have commonly led opponents to identify themselves with some system of belief. In the Second World War, the allies proclaimed themselves as upholders of freedom and democracy, by contrast with their fascist and totalitarian opponents. Similarly the struggle for national independence has produced an array of 'isms' thought suitable for national identification. Africans, for example, find themselves impelled to believe in anti-colonialism, neutralism, consciencism and African socialism, on pain of being thought traitors to the national cause. Many nations have therefore sought to equip themselves with a national doctrine or ideology which will perform the same intellectually unifying and distinguishing function as religion in past times. Ideologies of this kind are closely connected both with such national traditions as may exist, and also with the events of the struggle for independence. They are described as the 'philosophy of the Revolution', a form given to them by such popular leaders as Fidel Castro, Kwame Nkrumah and Gamal Nasser.

National symbols are a focus of pride in what they symbolise. And so far as group pride goes, all nations are in competition. This competition operates very obviously in the field of sport, where the numbers of gold medals won, the cups attained or the records broken, are reflected back into national awareness of proofs of its worth, significant of more than merely individual or team attainment. The Olympic Games, revived in 1896 as an arena in which hostile nations might meet in a politically neutralised atmosphere, have provoked a strenuous national effort by any country with a chance of shining. The most famous example of the subordination of sport to politics was the 1936 Olympic Games in Berlin, which the Nazi regime staged as a carnival of racialist doctrine. National worth is also furtively asserted in the various rumours and stories that purport to show the superior bravery or resourcefulness of a nation's soldiers. Or national intelligence may be implied in accounts of scientific and technical discoveries made by members of the nation. Most European countries can field an impressive team of men who have contributed to the growth of science, and all the large countries of Europe can 'claim' giants. Even here, however, we find nationalist confusions distorting the record. In the period before 1914, virtually every European country had men tinkering around with aeroplanes, internal combustion engines, and electrical devices of various kinds. The tendency of nationalist history is to demonstrate the nation's intelligence by irrelevant claims to priority in all possible fields.

These comparative evaluations are inevitably partial.

Language and the Threat to Uniqueness

A nation needs a literature—including some anonymous saga from bygone days and a gallery of talented writers in more recent times. The centrepiece of cultural nationalism is some dominating figure who can be cast in the role of the great national poet.[2] The first great national poet, Shakespeare, was established on his pedestal in the latter part of the eighteenth century largely by Germans in revolt against French classicism. Dante became the great Italian poet soon after, and for similarly oblique reasons. Dante thought of himself as something both more and less than an Italian: as a Christian and a Florentine. Cervantes, who came to stand for Spain in this gallery of national personages, was even less suitable, for part of his concern was to satirise rather than to glorify the Spanish character. And Goethe, who actually lived through the process of pedestalisation, fought back in his resentment at the use of literature to provoke discord between men. It is no doubt best if your national poet celebrates your national virtues but, in this field, distinction has to be taken where it is to be found, and nationalism takes the form of lopping off unsuitable sentiments here and highlighting convenient ones there.

By analogy, there is room for the nation's great painter, composer, sculptor, etc. Some modern composers, such as Sibelius in Finland, are prepared in some moods to accept this role, and to write appropriately nationalist works. But what of the countries who do not possess such figures? Here, once more, the deficiencies of the past can be corrected in the future: such countries wait for the great national novel or work of art; prizes are instituted, and artistic activities are encouraged as an aspect of national endeavour. Perhaps the most fortunate countries in this respect are those like the United States, where the steady output of many decades renders the quest for the 'great American novel' an absurdity. There is no 'great American novel' (though *Moby Dick* has sometimes been plausibly taken as such) but there is the work of Whitman (often a self-consciously nationalist poet), Hemingway, Faulkner, Dreiser, Henry James, Edgar Allan Poe, and all the rest, to demonstrate that a literature has arisen whilst men were looking for a book. In the United States, literary nationalism has been just one of those disconnected sentiments which never add up to a genuine nationalism. Few Americans, for example, can have regretted the fact of being burdened with the English tongue, which is also spoken in other countries; they have not worried that its implicit categories do violence to the American national soul. And there is a sense in which, again unwatched, American discourse has indeed developed into something quite distinct, while remaining a part of the English linguistic family.

A new nation that has no great artistic figures to its name can live on hope. But what if it does not have a language in which these great literary figures might write? This is the point where language, as a piece of national equipment, presents almost insoluble difficulties. We have already discussed Herder's insistence on language as the fundamental expression of a nation's soul. This strand of thinking is so strong that it looks at times as if the pure nationalist doctrine takes language as *the* key to the existence of a nation, all other criteria being secondary. That the nation should speak a unique language is necessary in order to facilitate internal communication, as well as to hinder external cultural influences. Underlying nationalism is the assumption that the nation-state is the *natural* and final political organisation of the world. Now if we have a country which speaks the same language or languages as those of powerful neighbours, then such a country's independent existence has the look of an accident due to diplomatic arrangements. Savoy has been at different times Italian and French; Navarre has been both Spanish and French; Schleswig has been both Danish and German. Such reshufflings of territory have been a commonplace of European politics. By this criterion, that indigestible datum of nationalist discussions, Switzerland, ought to be absorbed into Germany, France and Italy, leaving as a remainder only that tiny area which speaks Rumansh. But Switzerland has defied this criterion by a solidity which it has acquired from longstanding traditions.

The actual theory of nationalism might be saved from such difficulties by taking 'language' in a metaphorical sense. 'People who speak the same language' would then become, not necessarily those who use the same set of words, but those who, in some perhaps spiritual sense, understand each other. And many Swiss appear to have had the experience that, for example, if German-speaking, they are more at home with French-speaking Swiss than with German-speaking Austrians or Germans.[3] 'To speak the same language' in this metaphorical sense means loving the same things, admiring the same kinds of behaviour, sharing customs, and understanding each other's experiences. There is another dimension to this metaphorical usage. A language may be taken, not merely as a set of words and rules of syntax, not merely as a kind of emotional reciprocity, but also as a certain conceptualisation of the world. The culture of the twentieth century has been strongly marked by a thorough sensitivity to language, amounting among many English philosophers to the view that our beliefs are in many cases determined by language structure. Now each national soul is presumed to understand the world in a distinctive manner. A nation which speaks a foreign language seems therefore to have surrendered its unique understanding of the world to the attitudes of its cultural conquerors.

This theory that language is an essential piece of national equipment obviously gives rise to enormous difficulties when applied to the world. And these difficulties are even greater in the non-European world. We have seen the early German nationalists fearing that the German national soul was being submerged by the use of French in polite and literary intercourse. But German was a widespread language with an elaborate literature; it was, by contrast with the Celtic languages of the British Isles, quite unsinkable. Nationalism in Ireland, for example, led to a revival of, and a demand for the revival of, Gaelic. There was a renewed interest in Irish literature; nationalists who spoke the original language wore with pride a small badge called the *fainne*; and de Valera told his friends of the Gaelic League that if he had to choose between language and freedom, he would choose language. Edward de Valera transformed himself into Eamon de Valera. In the Irish Dail (=chamber of deputies) in 1927, he would begin speaking in Gaelic, only to be forced to revert to English by the fact that not all the deputies could understand him.[4] The teaching of Gaelic was made compulsory once Ireland had become independent. These legislative enactments amount to a nationalist demand for the revival of Gaelic, and it is a demand which has been very meagrely satisfied. Most Irishmen are much happier speaking English.

In Wales the language situation is almost the reverse of the Irish. The Welsh language had a considerable natural vitality which required preservation rather than revival. Welsh nationalism centres around the Welsh language not as one clause in a nationalist theory but as a stubborn defence of an already strong culture. The symbolic gestures—nationalists demanding legal documents or television licences in Welsh—amount to an attempt to prevent the fossilisation of the Welsh language as a result of the universal convenience of English in British administrative documents. Welsh nationalism combines the defence of a culture with the grievances of an economic region.

Grave difficulties arise where the nationalist theory of language collides with states in which no one language has an obviously dominating position. Belgium, for example, has suffered dissensions because it is divided into two strong groups, Flemings and Walloons. The central nucleus of Yugoslavia is the Serbian element, but this is not strong enough to impose uniformity throughout the country on the many linguistic minorities. For the language issue draws on all the other animosities within a mixed community, each element of which sees itself threatened.

In non-European countries, the situation is further complicated. In India, English became the one language uniting all those educated men who led the nationalist movement. They were led to it because during the British *raj* a command of English was the sole path of advancement; and they continued to use English, partly because educated Indians had no other common language, and partly because of its convenience in cultural and international affairs. The pressure of linguistic nationalism, however, opposed the continued diffusion of a foreign tongue, and Congress could at least agree that English should not remain the official language of India. But what was to replace it? India had hundreds of languages, belonging primarily to two distinct language groups, the Sanskrit-derived languages spoken in the north, and the Dravidian spoken in the south. Many of these languages had a considerable literature, but none was supplied with a technical vocabulary appropriate to a twentieth-century education. The solution made at the time of partition was that fourteen major Indian languages were accorded the status of 'official' languages. Hindi was to be the official language of all India, and English was to continue as an official language until 1965. But alliance is not amenable to legislative deadline.

The situation in most African states is broadly similar. None of the African tribal languages is in its present form a suitable vehicle for Westernisation and, except for Swahili, they are all limited to the tribal regions in which they originated. As in India, the educated middle classes of the various states can communicate only in English or French. Portuguese is the European language of Angola and Mozambique, and a legacy of Italian remains in Libya and parts of Somalia. But English and French dominate the continent; French because the colonial policy of France was dedicated to what was thought to be a civilising mission, and civilisation here meant French culture. The diffusion of English was less systematic, but has become just as widespread in former British colonies as French in the French community. Nationalist theory leads to a general agreement that autochthonous languages ought to be conserved and developed; on the other hand, no one can see any serious candidate for an indigenous African common language. Faced with this problem the Second Conference of Negro Writers and Artists meeting in Rome in 1959 resolved: 'The Commission on Literature hopes that Negro-African writers will work to define their common language, their common manner of using words and ideas and of reacting to them. The desire for an ordered language expressing coherent cultures is embodied, among other things, in work within a national reality from which the flagrant disorder specifically inherent in the colonial situation will be banished. This language, transcending the various languages used, transcending the legitimate forms of national cultures, will thus contribute towards strengthening the unity of the Negro peoples, and will furnish their writers with a working tool.'[5] The Commission, in other words, could see no solution to the problem, but hoped that something would turn up.

The nationalist theory of language is the focus for a variety of typical nationalist problems. We may consider two of them. In the first place, the replacement of a colonial language by an indigenous one involves conflicting interests. One kind of intellectual capital, namely a knowledge of English or French, becomes more or less obsolete, whilst another form of capital, knowledge of the native language, correspondingly appreciates. By legislative enactment, a vast market opens up for books and translations, and a new class of intellectuals comes into existence. As the language becomes diffused throughout the society, local writers and journalists come to possess a more or less captive market for their literature. Once more, language is made ready for its great national writer. We saw that this kind of motive operated in early German nationalism. In modern times, to promote a language in this way amounts to an enormous and expensive capital investment—in teachers, gramophone records, libraries, textbooks and publishing equipment. It begins to cut a culture off from the modern world at just the moment when national endeavour is bent on modernisation. The linguistic theory of nationalism and the demands of modernisation may thus come into radical conflict. Why is it often thought worth such sacrifices to develop a national language?

The answers to this are complex and partly speculative. Modernisation involves the imitation of Western models, primarily in technology but inevitably in much more. The policy of imitation here points in two directions: should the nation adopt also a European language in its cultural affairs? Many of these new nations already have such a language bequeathed to them from the colonial period. Or should they imitate the larger states in having a language of their own? The second conclusion is the one that appeals to the consistent nationalist.

But beyond this there looms an important fear which Negro writers have termed 'loss of personality'. In using English or French, they fear that they will become simply Black Englishmen or Black Frenchmen, and this would be to give up the uniqueness on which they base their demand for a special place in the world. They would be doomed forever to an alien mode of being. This is a part of the concern which led Gandhi to advocate cottage industry, and to resist industrialisation. Working in factories, Indians, it was thought, would eventually develop not merely the activities but the same spirit as Europeans. Similarly, the Irish revival of Gaelic has a lot to do with keeping Irishmen from turning into Englishmen with a funny accent.

It is worth asking: how real is this fear? And the answer is complicated by the vagueness of the issue involved. The Westernisation of large parts of the world has certainly meant the end of many customs, some of them, like footbinding, *suttee* and *purdah*, not to be greatly regretted. It has also involved the importation of some unlovely types of behaviour such as juvenile delinquency and the commercialisation of social relations. But these changes come in the context of a broadly consistent and at least for the moment irreversible decision to participate in the Westernised world of economics and technology. That modernisation has had, and will undoubtedly continue to have, quite unpredictable consequences. The one certain thing is that the consequences will not be uniform. We can only imagine that they will be so if we look at the matter abstractly. Doctors in different parts of the world lack the quaint variety of witchdoctors and *shamans*, but they are very far from being identical robots. The English-speaking states may almost be regarded as a laboratory experiment on this question, and although they are composed of people largely of common stock, and certainly speaking a common language, they have not failed, in a very short time, to develop a highly concentrated sense of national differences.

The nationalist belief that a language expresses the soul of a nation is a piece of mysticism difficult to construe rationally. It may be true that certain languages are more suitable for some operations than others: French is credited with clarity, but this does not prevent intellectual confusion among the French. Italian sounds like poetry and is splendidly suitable for operatic libretti, but there is plenty of ugly discourse among Italians. The language that one uses has always been, among both the very sophisticated and the unfortunate, a matter of choice. The unfortunate are the millions of people who emigrate and change their language in their lifetime. The sophisticated have often chosen another language as a vehicle of self-expression. The Pole Conrad wrote novels in English; the Irishman Beckett writes plays in French. Nigerians and Indians have available to them both their local language, and also English; and many of them choose to write in English. They do so partly for reasons of circulation, and partly for artistic reasons. But what they produce has, even in English, a character of its own. Hence one answer, only mildly tendentious, to the charge that an English-speaking uniformity is spreading through large areas of the world is George Bernard Shaw's epigram that the British and Americans are divided by a common language.

The Political Implications of Independence

Nationalist movements strive for freedom and self-government. But what is freedom? The minimal meaning in this context is: freedom is what happens when the foreign rulers leave. Often unrealistic hopes have been concentrated upon that long-desired event, and political leaders moderate their rhetoric as it approaches. The fate of different classes in the new nation will vary. For the successful political class, freedom does indeed mean concrete things: chauffeur-driven cars, large offices, appointments in rich foreign capitals, and so on. A big part of equality between nations is how leaders live. For most of the population, freedom means very little in the way of immediate improvement. To the extent that they felt humiliated by foreign rule, they may hold their heads higher. It was reported that when Ghana became independent, Ghanaian players attributed their football victories over Nigeria to the magic of independence. But for a number of reasons, ranging from rapid population growth to simple mismanagement, the economic lot of peasant and proletarian has often worsened. And in recent years, it has coincidentally happened that the terms of trade have turned against primary producing countries, making matters even worse. This is a lottery encouraging rapid diversification; the cocoa of West Africa brings in less, the copper of Zambia brings in more.

Self-government is a vague term even when we are dealing with a homogeneous nation. It always means some kind of majority rule, inevitably suiting some more than others. But what when that majority is racially or culturally distinct from the minorities of the new state? The great virtue of a colonial regime, so far as minorities are concerned, is that it stands above the local battle. Once this regime is removed, local enmities may have free play. In some new nations, this has been the initial meaning of independence. Consequently, joy at independence was often rather muted among tribes like the Ashanti in Ghana, or the Muslims living in India, among the Chinese in Malaysia, and Asians (generally Indians) in East Africa.

The theory of nationalism was not made to fit situations of this kind; it might suggest two possibilities. A country like Kenya, for example, might be taken as fundamentally Kikuyu (for the Kikuyu are the largest tribe), or as fundamentally black (for Africans far outnumber all other races). If so, then whites and Asians are foreigners permitted to live in the nation's territory so long as it is convenient. Alternatively, Kenya might be taken in its present mixed condition, and an attempt be made to hammer out something that might be called a Kenyan nation. This latter policy, whose success depends on the steady diminution of tribal and communal animosities, is the one which Kenya's first government, led by Jomo Kenyatta, chose to follow. The difficulty of the whole idea of nationalism in such a context as this is that we find a variety of things which all seem to have the same claim to be called nationalism: there is black nationalism within Kenya, Kenyan nationalism as practised by Kenyatta, and there is pan-Africanism. Nationalism here describes a form of group self-assertion qualified in terms of the group on whose behalf it is practised. And it should be clear that the term nationalism has been stretched so thin as to become uninformative.

The political equipment of a new nation composed of several peoples must begin with a constitution. A constitution is an instrument by which settled and peaceful procedures may govern the political life of a state. The prototype of all modern constitutions is the first and most successful—that of the United States. They are generally liberal documents which guarantee rights to the population at large, express some kind of ideological attachment to God and progress, and provide for the circumstances in which the constitution may be suspended and amended. Much in non-European constitutions is an imitation of the West, and is irrelevant to current Afro-Asian politics, but the provisions determining the suspension and amendment of a constitution are the crux of nationalist politics. Constitutions emerge usually from detailed and difficult bargaining in the period immediately preceding independence, and their structure is the price paid by the dominant race or people in order to attain some kind of consensus about independence. For in many cases the minorities are distrustful of imminent majority rule, and must be wooed with guarantees. Such is the situation in countries as disparate as Kenya and Malaysia.

Setting up the apparatus of a new state presents us, as often in politics, with a mixture of logical and social considerations. In nearly all newly independent states, the campaign for independence has been fought under the slogans of democracy. The main point of the slogan is to enforce the principle of one-man, one-vote, and thereby bring the local leaders to power. But the implications of democracy include according the rights of citizenship to all who live permanently within the state. Logic therefore seems to dictate a policy of allowing entrenched rights to minorities. It is also politically necessary to agree to such rights because otherwise independence is likely to be threatened or at least delayed. Further, there are usually hopes that in future people will act differently from the way they have acted in the past. All of these considerations run counter to what would seem to be the purest pronouncement of nationalism on this point: that minorities are not to be tolerated. The logic of nationalism leads to the massive transfer of populations so that citizenship coincides precisely with nationality. Sometimes the attitudes of nationalists or the fear experienced by minorities has led many people to flee the new state. But on this point, the leaders of new nations are commonly flexible; and at least their early intentions are to allow a good deal of freedom to the various ethnic groups over which they will rule.

A further difficulty arises. Democracy requires an opposition. Most inheritor-states of the British Empire, for example, have established what has come to be known as the Westminster model of democracy, a system of procedures which are only sensible if there is a two-party system. And a two-party system involves the existence of an opposition. Given an ethnically plural society, the commonest form of political alignment is for the minorities to constitute the opposition. But an opposition of this kind is very different from the kind of opposition found in Britain and America. European oppositions commonly hope in time to take over the government. While they are sometimes based upon social class, they consist of loose alliances of voters who share many common interests with their political opponents. All parties usually believe that it is more important to keep the system going than to win any single political issue; and the leaders of both government and opposition usually have sufficient tactical skill to prevent issues arising which will lead any section of the community to desperation. There are, of course, occasional exceptions to this—the problem of Ireland in British politics up to 1922; that of race relations in the deep South of the United States—and they illustrate the difficulties of this form of politics.

Now in a poly-ethnic society, the situation is quite different, and we have already encountered the Muslims of India drawing the conclusion that they must establish a separate state. In these societies, we have an opposition which *is* liable to feel desperation every time a political crisis arises. It is always difficult to draw a distinction between a 'loyal opposition' and a treasonous coterie. A tradition of public violence and a disposition to interpret politics in terms of conspiracies—a disposition encouraged by nationalist ideology itself —will soon render Westminster-style democracy impossible. The common phrase of the moment is to say that this style of democracy is not 'appropriate to African (or Asian, etc.) realities'. The implication is that there are other forms of democracy which are appropriate. But on this issue, as on many, we are involved in a form of modern cant. There is certainly no reason why non-European nations should follow the details of what is done in Westminster or Washington; there is equally no reason to pretend that many of the alternatives they have found must be called 'democratic', a word which sinks ever lower towards the horizon of meaninglessness. Most Afro-Asian countries are ruled in a more or less authoritarian way, as indeed they must be where the mass of the population is largely unaccustomed to political participation and lacks the habits of democratic moderation.

There are, of course, exceptions to this. India has succeeded in running a large-scale democracy along broadly traditional lines; and in Tanzania the magnetic personality of Mr Nyerere for the present sustains a form of popular consultation which it would be no violation of language to call 'democratic'. Maintaining democracy where the nation is bent on modernisation has considerable political advantages, but we would be unwise to make a fetish out of either the word or the institution. Perhaps it is salutary to remember that many of the achievements of civilisation have been produced under authoritarian political systems.

A new nation needs a head of state. Among nineteenth-century nationalists, a prince was thought indispensable. The Italians had a local candidate, the Germans had a variety of possibilities; but even in countries like Rumania and Greece, entirely lacking in royalty, the need was felt. New job-opportunities opened up for unemployed German princelings. Rumania imported a Prussian prince, Greece managed to get through two of them, in the course of the century. When princes went out of fashion, dictators came in. The period between 1919 and 1939 was the time of strong, indeed strident, heads of state ready to claim 'I am the state'. In the post-war period, nearly every successful nationalist movement was headed by a strong personality. The history of this period is written in the names— Nehru, Sukarno, Nasser, Nkrumah, Castro, Ben Bella, etc. They were usually men of great ability, and generally also of great charm. Above all, they had 'dynamism', which is to political leaders what star-quality is to actors. In states where the identity of the nation was fluid and indeterminate, their acts and pronouncements incarnated the national spirit, and gave to politics just the flamboyance needed to sustain the attention of populations in the process of emerging from the narrow preoccupations of the village. On the other hand, they were usually strong-willed and impatient of opposition; some of them took to symbolising the nation with gestures so expensive as to run the state into bankruptcy. The result was that in many countries —Indonesia, Ghana, Algeria, for example—the flamboyant national leader was followed by a regime of retrenchment often run by soldiers.

Newly independent states have both a foreign and domestic policy to wage. In formulating a foreign policy, they find themselves immediately drawn into the world political scene. They immediately acquire seats in the United Nations, and there are few pieces of territory so remote and valueless as to be of no consequence to the far-flung preoccupations of the Americans or of Russian or Chinese communists. This situation contrasts with the position of small and relatively powerless states in earlier times. A Liberia or an Afghanistan was in those times a factor of no political consequence. Modern states are also commonly involved in further groupings like the Commonwealth or the Community. They learn quickly how they may play off one side against the other, and encourage the receipt of various forms of aid. In many cases this kind of foreign policy does not exhaust the political momentum of the independence movement which floated them to nationhood. Among African nations, for example, there is the considerable preoccupation with building up an African state, and arranging the regional co-operation which may be seen as advances along that road. Again, the nation may express itself at the many conferences at which Afro-Asian nations take up positions on world events and pass resolutions.

The domestic policy of new states is dominated by two general issues. The first of these is the maintenance of the nation itself. We have seen that minority groups usually manage to get guarantees of a right to some degree of autonomy, but their position remains insecure. The Chinese in Indonesia, Asians and Europeans in African states, Kurds in Iraq, Chinese and Indians in Malaysia, Karens and Shans in Burma—the list of troubled or troublesome minorities is very long, and is intimately involved with civil war, actual or potential. These problems are not, of course, limited to new nations; they are to be found in the best-established states. The French in Canada, the Welsh in Great Britain, the Catalans in Spain, each of these is an example of nationalist minorities constituting a problem for the government that rules them. This is one of the cases where economic and nationalist aspirations run directly counter to each other. Economic pressures are generally towards increasingly large units, and render dreams of nationalist autarchy increasingly unreal. Ironically enough, the purest solution to the nationalist problem, next to the forcible transfer of population, is to be found in something like the South African system of *apartheid*. Here each people—Bantu,

Xosa, Coloureds and Whites—is in principle accorded its own area for development. This accords well with pure nationalist doctrine. But there are, of course, qualifications. For one thing, in nationalist terms the white population of South Africa is two nations, for there are two languages. The theological racialism of the Union, however, recognises only Europeans. Further, the 'separate development' of the non-white peoples is under the restrictive direction of the appropriately named Nationalist Party. But South Africa is typical of other areas at least in the fact that the economic links between all sections of the population undermine the rationalist conception of a South Africa composed of pools of racial purity under white hegemony.

Most of the new nations are also underdeveloped economically. Competition between ethnic groups for severely limited resources and jobs adds an extra element of instability to an already difficult situation. The leaders of these countries consequently take the view that the only long-term solution for many of their political problems is the rapid modernisation of their economies. This view may not always be strictly correct; there has been plenty of political tension in rich countries, as the history of twentieth-century Europe teaches us. But apart from the hope that affluence will solve political problems, nationalist leaders find it inherently worthwhile to try to divert the energies of their subjects from the fruitless communal animosities of the past into the war against poverty, a struggle which promises far more. The politics of modern nationalism is therefore the politics of underdevelopment; and as such, it may transform nationalist politics into something more familiar to contemporary Western experience.

To develop an economy is to acquire another important part of the equipment of a proper nation. In Europe the process took centuries; each of the new nations seeks to do it with the utmost rapidity. And in a nationalist atmosphere, this leads to a number of characteristic vices. The central vice is to believe that national development is a matter of national *will*; but a modern economy is built up by thousands of individuals pursuing personal rather than national politics; national development, that is to say, is a by-product of individual endeavour. National development by will leads to events like the Russian collectivisation of agriculture in 1930, or the Chinese Great Leap Forward, attempts to annihilate time which frequently cause further delay. An associated vice of a nationalist atmosphere is a disposition to take the plan for the achievement.[6] Economic planning, like many other useful things, can become the vehicle of compensatory fantasies. And a further economic vice is a disposition to concentrate upon symbols: the passion for a steelworks, the empty Boeing 707 on scheduled flights for the national airline, the skyscrapers in the desert. All of these vices are the results of sheer desperation, the passion that many nationalists have invested in the process of becoming a proper nation.

But what is a proper nation? The problem here is that it is a little like a mirage in the desert—it is always just ahead. A proper nation can be seen in terms of modernisation, what happens when a traditional society has given way to a literate and urbanised society. But even modernisation is a changing ideal. We hinted in discussing the various heads of state—princes, leaders, generals—that there was an element of fashion in these things. Obviously each country has its own unique circumstances which determined its political evolution, and nationalist politics is not like a dance in which the beat changes all at once. But when all this is said, there remains the factor of imitation. Balkan countries, looking at the world of their time, decided that a prince was necessary to statehood, because most of the great powers had princes. Later the demagogic style of politics aroused the enthusiasm, and promised to solve the problems, of the newer generations of student politicians. And still later, the military overthrow of leaders too expensive for the country to support was an expedient whose use in one country suggested a solution to problems in another. Nationalism is one country learning from another—sometimes without discrimination.

6

Explanations of Nationalism

Let us now turn away from nationalist thought and devote ourselves to thought about nationalism. We may distinguish two kinds. Firstly, there are the attitudes which other ideologies have developed towards nationalism. Since each ideology has to compete for the allegiance of its followers, it must supply some account of the errors of its competitors. We shall discuss two cases of this kind of ideological friction—involving liberalism and Marxism. Secondly, there are the attempts scholars make to understand nationalism as a part of the universe we live in. Historians try to exhibit nationalism as a natural outcome of preceding events. Social scientists often try to discover the causes of nationalism, assuming it to be a single class of phenomena which can be grouped together for purposes of explanation. And philosophers attempt to explain nationalism as an intellectual system belonging to an ordered universe.

Ideological Friction: Liberalism

English liberals first encountered nationalism in the form of the principle of nationality, a principle which seemed to them eminently rational. English politicians of most persuasions felt that the partition of Poland in the eighteenth century was an indefensible act of dynastic violence.[1] Their sympathies were subsequently aroused by the struggles of the Greeks against Ottoman domination, the Belgians against Holland, and the Italians and Hungarians against Hapsburg rule. They found Mazzini, who spent many years of exile in England, a sympathetic figure, and they were inclined to agree with his view that political instability resulted from dynastic despotism and that it would disappear when the political structure of Europe coincided with the national. John Stuart Mill wrote in 1861: 'Where the sentiment of nationality exists in any force, there is a *prima facie* case for uniting all the members of the nationality under the same government, and a government to themselves apart.'[2] He justifies this assertion in the next sentence: 'This is merely saying that the question of government ought to be decided by the governed.' In other words, Mill identified the principle of nationality as a clause of liberalism itself. Nineteenth-century Englishmen opposed the great multi-national despotisms of the Continent. Associating multi-national empires with despotism, they naturally concluded that national states would be liberal.

This simple logical relationship ceases to be plausible the moment one looks at actual political behaviour. Nationalists always present themselves as a movement of the weak against the strong, and therefore solicit our support for the underdog in an unequal struggle. Support for this attitude, common to liberals the world over, has continued up to the present day. In the twentieth century, liberal sympathy has embraced nationalist movements throughout the Afro-Asian world. Whereas conservatives have steadily granted freedom to colonial dependencies on the principle that if someone is about to smash down a door, the sensible thing is to open it up and let him in, liberals have supported the same policy on the grounds that they think it right. Indeed, the nationalist emphasis upon 'freedom' as a political objective is partly conditioned by the aim of appealing for sympathy to liberal groups in the colonising country. So long as nationalism looks like a special case of the demand for freedom, then liberals, softened up by arguments based on exploitation and the corruptions of power, will listen sympathetically.

Yet the year after Mill's *Considerations*, the liberal historian, Acton, wrote his famous essay on nationality. By 1862, it was already clear to an acute observer such as Acton that nationality, far from being an ally of liberalism, was directly opposed to it. He recognised that it was both revolutionary and despotic in character. He also observed its extreme fluidity. Thinking of Italy, he wrote: 'The same spirit served different masters, and contributed first to the destruction of the old States, then to the expulsion of the French, and again, under Charles Albert, to a new revolution. It was appealed to in the name of the most contradictory principles of government, and served all parties in succession, because it was one in which all could unite.'[3] Nationalism is, in other words, not the belief in a principle of government on all-fours with liberalism, but a quite different kind of thing, to be distinguished as a spirit or style of politics. Acton took Mazzini's life as a paradigm of the development of the principle, 'Exile is the nursery of nationality, as oppression is the school of liberalism.'

The tenor of Acton's argument is such that English liberals and conservatives alike might unite in supporting it. We have already made clear, in the discussion of Germany, that nationalism is a force which seeks a radical transformation of politics; it is hostile to long-established institutions and connections. It is therefore a direct enemy of conservative politics. This point is worth emphasising, for there are many writers who impose upon politics little more than the impoverished distinction between the left wing and the right wing. In nineteenth-century Europe, observing that socialism had taken over the position of the left wing, they concluded that nationalism must be right-wing and (by a slippery transition of ideas) consequently conservative. This judgment was also supported by pointing to the use made of nationalist slogans by the fascist movements which prospered in Europe between 1919 and 1939, for fascism is usually taken as 'right-wing'. But the central point about nationalism is Acton's 'the same spirit served different masters', and having grasped this, we shall abandon any attempt to fit nationalism somewhere on a left–right scale.

The hinge of Acton's argument is a discussion of patriotism which depends upon a distinction between the state and the nation. Our attachment to the nation is natural and material; patriotism is the development of the instinct of self-preservation into a *moral* duty which may require the sacrifice of our private interests or even of life itself. This transformation is something achieved by the state, which cannot be identified with the nation in any natural sense. Acton supported this argument by recourse to Burke's distinction between the moral and the natural country, a distinction implied when Burke remarks: 'France is out of itself—the moral France is separated from the geographical.' Those Frenchmen who fought against revolutionary France might thus, in Burke's view, be described as patriots; and for a modern analogue, we might take the case of Germans who resisted the Nazi regime. It is on the basis of such reasoning that Acton declares the principle of nationality to be both criminal and absurd.

His argument is perfectly general and applicable to much more than nationalism: 'Whenever a single definite object is made the supreme end of the State, be it the advantage of a class, the safety or the power of the country, the greatest happiness of the greatest number, or the support of any speculative idea, the State becomes for a time inevitably absolute.' And his conclusion from this premise is one of the standing beliefs of liberalism: 'The co-existence of several nations under the same State is a test, as well as the best security of its freedom. It is also one of the chief instruments of civilisation; and, as such, it is in the natural and providential order, and indicates a state of greater advancement than the national unity which is the ideal of modern liberalism.'

Acton recognises that to affirm the principle of nationality is an option open to liberals; and in this quotation he implies that most liberals have taken up the option. We have seen that they have continued to do so when considering colonial situations. Yet the other strand of liberalism, which Acton himself espouses, was in the long run to dominate liberal thought. Acton thinks in terms of the progress of civilisation, a criterion adopted even more uncritically by John Stuart Mill. Mill, as we saw, supported the principle of nationality because he associated it with liberty. But in the same chapter he can write: 'Nobody can suppose that it is not more beneficial to a Breton, or a Basque of French Navarre, to be brought into the current of the ideas and feeling of a highly civilised and cultivated people—to be a member of the French nationality, admitted on equal terms to all the privileges of French citizenship, sharing the advantages of French protection, and the dignity and prestige of French power—than to sulk on his own rocks, the half-savage relic of past times, revolving in his own little mental orbit, without participation or interest in the general movement of the world.'[4] Mill supplies us with two relevant principles: a support of nationality where it breaks up despotic empires, in accordance with the wishes of the people; and an overriding concern with the general progress of civilisation.

These two principles might logically, and did historically, conflict with each other. The kind of situation where the conflict tore at the consciences of English liberals was to be found in Ireland, and in South Africa. Some liberals supported the rights of small nationalities, struggling, as it seemed, to be free. The irony of Afrikaners struggling to be free only became fully evident in the course of the next half-century. But even in the less ambiguous case of Ireland, a liberal-minded man like Sidney Webb did not appear to have much doubt: 'We at any rate', he wrote in Fabian tract 108, 'are precluded from assuming or admitting that any distinct "nationality", just because it imagines itself to have ends which differ from, and perhaps conflict with, the common interests of the Empire as a whole, has, therefore, an abstract right to organise an independent government and pursue those ends at whatever cost to its colleagues or neighbours.'[5]

In the twentieth century the principle of nationality came to be described as national self-determination, and retained sufficient support among liberals to be the favoured panacea of Woodrow Wilson and (with less enthusiasm and single-mindedness) his allies who redrew the map of Europe in 1919. The Austro-Hungarian Empire was broken up and replaced by independent nation-states like Austria, Czechoslovakia, Hungary, and the enlarged Serbia that became Yugoslavia. Each of these nations contained large minorities, averaging, it has been estimated, about 30 per cent of their total populations. The paradox was that a political settlement designed to fulfil the aspirations of smaller nationalities had succeeded in creating an intolerable situation for millions of people: for it is a much worse fate to live as part of a minority in a nationalist state than to be one people among many ruled by a multi-national empire, even if that empire is somewhat despotic. Eastern Europe remained a source of political instability, and a *reductio ad absurdum* of the principle of nationality.

The modern liberal position arises from the prominence of the concept of aggression in liberal thought. Threats to peace in the twentieth century were presumed to result from aggression, the cause of which was nationalism. Liberals were therefore in the vanguard of those proclaiming that national sovereignty had become, in an era of powerful weapons, not merely an anachronism but a dangerous anachronism. They looked forward to the steady growth of, first the League of Nations, later the United Nations, as both the expression of a world public opinion and as an authoritative arbiter in the international disputes which had previously led to armed conflict.

But within this general position, liberals allowed the colonial area as one in which a people's national aspirations had a right to press onwards to the creation of nation-states; and a great deal of indulgence was accorded to post-war nationalist movements, as though they constituted a sort of political puberty terminating in full and responsible membership of the community of nations.

Nationalism and Marxism

In 1848, when Karl Marx was 30, he and Engels published the *Communist Manifesto*. 'A spectre is haunting Europe', the *Manifesto* declared. It was indeed true that the rulers of Europe were not sleeping well in the year or two following 1848, but it was hardly Marx who was keeping them awake. It is even true that they were haunted by the fear of revolution; but revolutions can be made for all manner of purposes, and the revolutions made around 1848—in Vienna, Paris, Frankfurt, Budapest and in Italy—were all predominantly nationalist. The notion that the workers would rise up and expropriate the expropriators was a remote possibility only in Paris, where in 1848 the scheme of Louis Blanc for public workshops had a brief moment of strangled glory before normalcy, in the form of Louis Napoleon, reasserted itself. The *Manifesto* at the time it was written was an intelligent piece of bluff. In a turmoil of small and quarrelsome groups, one faction had had the brilliant idea of bidding for attention with the cry: *We* are the real opposition. For Marx and Engels realised that what would make the fortunes of their group would be the concentrated enmity of the rulers and the rich of Europe.

Marxism and nationalism are both revolutionary doctrines, and to that extent they can co-operate in attacks upon the *status quo*. They are both doctrines of struggle, but they diverge fundamentally on the nature of the struggle. Marxism vertically divided the world into exploiters and exploited; nationalism horizontally cut it into many distinct nationalities. In the middle of the nineteenth century the apostles of these two creeds, the near-contemporaries Marx and Mazzini, were both living in exile in London. There is no doubt that compared with Marx, Mazzini was a woolly-minded incompetent. Yet, equally it seems that, if torn between attachment to a socialist future or attachment to one's own nation, most men have chosen to stay with their own. Nationalism in the period before 1914 was instrumental in making a number of states; communism up to 1917 had failed to tear one down.

The gap between socialist aspirations and patriotic reality opened up dramatically in 1914. On 25 July 1914, on the eve of the First World War, the Executive Committee of the German Social Democratic Party proclaimed: 'No German soldier's blood must be spilt to gratify the murderous intentions of the Austrian tyrant. We call upon you, comrades, to express at once by mass meetings the unshakable desire of the class-conscious proletariat for peace.'[6] Within a month, the party in the German *Reichstag* had voted in favour of German war-credits. Lenin, in Cracow at the time, at first refused to believe it, thinking that the capitalist press had invented Social Democratic support for the war. But the difficulty facing Marxists was that impeccably proletarian reasoning might lead to patriotic conclusions: the German social democrats could argue that a Tsarist victory would put back the socialist cause, whilst the Russian socialists could believe that a German victory would lead to the annexation of Russian territory and the loss to Russia of many areas where they were strongest. The premise assumed in both cases is that the proletarian parties of the other countries would be unable to cripple their own country's war effort.

The success of the Bolsheviks in taking over Russia in 1917 was, in terms of Marxist theory, an anomaly. For they found themselves in possession of a backward country where capitalism was weak, in exact defiance of the theory that the revolution would start among the proletariat of the most advanced countries of Western Europe. Russian policy after 1920 accepted as a tactical expedient the policy of building socialism in one country, and declared that the Soviet Union was the homeland of all true proletarians—an attempt to turn all patriotism into an attachment to Russia itself.

When, in 1941, German troops invaded Russia, Stalin was quick
to make the maximum use of Russian patriotic feeling, and to
emphasise, contrary to much previous teaching, the continuity
between the present Russian struggle, and the battles of Russian
national heroes like Alexander Nevsky and Mikhail Kutuzov. And
during the battle of Moscow, Stalin is reported to have said: 'Can
the Hitlerites be regarded as *nationalists*? No, they cannot. Actually,
the Hitlerites are now not nationalists but *imperialists*.' This amounts
to saying, as Deutscher points out: 'It is *we*, not our enemies, who are
the real nationalists.'[7]

This was a reversal of attitude at least to the extent that Marxists
had not hitherto regarded 'nationalist' as a good label to have. Yet
Stalin had, more than the other leaders of communism, taken an
interest in the nationalities question, which dated back to 1913
when he wrote *Marxism and the National Question*. This work was
written for directly political purposes, though its language and
structure are marked by the philosophical manner and vocabulary
common in Marxist work. It purports to be a work of commentary
on Marx, whose writings supply little for a writer on nationalism to
use. However, Stalin quotes with approval a few phrases from the
Communist Manifesto—'national differences and antagonisms between
peoples are vanishing gradually from day to day' and 'the supremacy
of the proletariat will cause them to vanish still faster'. He added
piously: 'The subsequent development of mankind, accompanied as
it was by the colossal growth of capitalist production, the shuffling
of nationalities, and the amalgamation of people within ever larger
territories, emphatically corroborates Marx's thought.'[8] But this, of
course, is quite untrue; even in established states like Britain and
Canada, nationalist feeling has displayed a surprising tenacity. And
feelings which we can only describe as nationalist have also played
havoc with the economic rationalisation of the communist world
itself. The Eastern economic bloc established by Stalin after 1945 has
broken down under pressure from nationalist decisions in Poland,
Rumania and other countries of the bloc. And China and Russia
have been alienated from each other by attitudes which seem entirely
nationalist, however much they may be camouflaged by disputes
about Marxist doctrinal orthodoxy.

The problem for a Marxist ideologist is to explain everything that comes within his range of thought in terms of the conceptual apparatus of Marxism. To a large extent, this is a simple matter of deciding whether a thing is good or bad; if good it must be linked with the 'proletariat', if bad with the bourgeoisie. Since policies may have to be changed, these interpretations have to be reversible, and therefore allocations to different pigeonholes must be accompanied by suitable qualifications. And the allocation must be done on the basis of a variable mixture of logic and history. In this way, Stalinist policy towards 'popular fronts' turned a number of notable somersaults in the 1930s, and attitudes towards colonial nationalist movements have been extremely flexible since 1945. Since nationalism has often competed with communism for popular support, it must be attacked; yet since on many occasions nationalist movements (especially in colonies) can serve communist purposes, the door of equivocation must be left open.

Stalin therefore sees nationalism within the context of capitalism: 'A nation is not merely a historical category but a historical category belonging to a definite epoch, the epoch of rising capitalism. The process of elimination of feudalism and development of capitalism was at the same time a process of amalgamation of people into nations.' The leading role in this process is played by the bourgeoisie. 'The chief problem for the young bourgeoisie is the problem of the market. Its aim is to sell its goods and to emerge victorious from competition with the bourgeoisie of another nationality. Hence its desire to secure its "own", its "home" market. The market is the first school in which the bourgeoisie learns its nationalism.'[9]

Is this true? It appears to be describing a historical process; but it is difficult to see what economic interests or even market preoccupations moved Herder or Fichte or Schleiermacher to their nationalist opinions. Stalin's account of the matter is Marxist in assuming that economic interests determine the course of historical events; and no doubt many, though not all, members of the bourgeoisie can make economic gains as the result of establishing a protected home market. But what the theory really needs for plausibility is the fact that *only* the bourgeoisie should benefit. What we commonly find, on the contrary, is that workers' parties are as nationalist as any bourgeois in their support for the development of local industry by tariff protection.

In order to get around this difficulty Stalin has to try to show that the 'higher' interests of the proletariat run contrary to those of developing nationalism. His view is that a 'good' proletariat will not be nationalist, but the way he puts this is to say: 'Whether the proletariat rallies to the banner of bourgeois nationalism depends on the degree of development of class contradictions, on the class-consciousness and degree of organisation of the proletariat. A class-conscious proletariat has its own tried banner, and it does not need to march under the banner of the bourgeoisie.' In other words, if Marxist parties are strong, nationalist parties will be weak; which is no doubt true.

But Stalin, we must remember, was a Georgian, a member of an oppressed nationality; and in 1913 the nationalities question was a sensitive area of Russian politics. He dealt with the question in a flexible manner by combining a complete capitulation to the principle of nationality with a qualification capable of nullifying this capitulation. First he agrees:

> But the workers are interested in the complete amalgamation of all their comrades into a single international army, in their speedy and final emancipation from intellectual subjection to the bourgeoisie, and in the full and free development of the intellectual forces of their brothers, whatever the nation to which they belong.
>
> Social-Democratic parties in all countries therefore proclaim the right of nations to self-determination.
>
> The right of self-determination means that only the nation itself has the right to determine its destiny, that no one has the right forcibly to interfere in the life of the nation, to destroy its schools and other institutions, to violate its habits and customs, to repress its language, or curtail its rights.

So far so good. This kind of rhetoric is enough to allow comrades to arrive at any kind of tactical accommodation they like with nationalists. But—

> This, of course, does not mean that Social-Democrats will support every custom and institution of a nation. While combating

the exercise of violence against any nation, they will only support the right of the nation to determine its own destiny, at the same time agitating against the noxious customs and institutions of that nation in order to enable the toiling strata of the nation to emancipate themselves from them. . . .

This of course does not mean that Social-Democrats will support every demand of a nation. A nation has the right even to return to the old order of things; but this does not mean that Social-Democrats will subscribe to such a decision if taken by any institution of the said nation. The obligations of Social-Democrats who defend the interests of the proletariat, and the rights of a nation, which consists of various classes, are two different things.[10]

The events of the last few decades have induced in most politically sophisticated people a highly cynical attitude to words of this kind. The later fate of Georgians, Ukrainians, and especially people like the Chechens who collaborated with the German army which invaded Russia in 1941, would seem to display the unreality, if not the hypocrisy of much that Stalin and other Marxists have said on the problems arising from nationalism. Yet it seems certain that these sentiments were entirely sincere. Early in 1918, which for Bolsheviks was one of those moments in human history when 'bliss was it in that dawn to be alive', the newly established Bolshevik government of Russia granted national independence to the Finns, and Stalin, the Commissar of Nationalities, turned up in Helsinki to declare a new era in which Tsarist expansionism would be a thing of the past. 'Full freedom to shape their own life is given to the Finns as well as to the other peoples of Russia!' Stalin then proclaimed: 'A voluntary and honest alliance between the Finnish and the Russian people! These are the guiding principles of the policy of the Council of People's Commissars.'[11] Guiding principles they may have been, but they very quickly got lost in the morass of political confusion consequent upon civil war and foreign attack that plagued Russia for the next three years. Bolshevik policy was immediately attacked on the grounds that it gave governmental powers to the Finnish bourgeoisie. And the policy ran into further difficulties when the Ukrainian *Rada*, dominated by Simon Petlura, demanded the recall of Ukrainian soldiers from the Russian army, and refused to allow Red troops through Ukrainian territory to defend the Donetz coal mines from White Russian attack by the armies of General Kaledin.

Both principle and policy were rapidly revised. The *Rada,* or Ukrainian nationalist assembly, was dispersed by Soviet troops, and the All-Russian Congress of Soviets declared that the principles of self-determination for the small nations 'ought to be understood as the right of self-determination not of the bourgeoisie but of the toiling masses of a given nation'.[12] A genuine concern for at least cultural autonomy in the various nationalist republics of the Soviet Union remained, combined with a clear refusal to allow the break-up of the multi-national empire which the Bolsheviks had inherited.

Attempts to Understand Nationalism

An ideologist is like a shopkeeper bound to keep only one brand of goods; whatever he says is suspect because we know that for him some conclusions are fixed beyond argument. This is the reason why, although ideological friction may generate highly intelligent discussions of nationalism, the arguments involved will always have a significantly different character from academic work. The Marxist association between nationalism and the bourgeoisie is a suggestive one and it is on the verge of being a scientific hypothesis; but we know that its truth for the Marxists is actually guaranteed by the logic of the ideology, and that it would not, in the form in which the ideologist presents it, be subjected to any serious testing.

One of the more open-minded ways of explaining nationalism is in terms of its history. But the difficulty here, as we suggested in Chapter 1, is that nationalism, as such, does not have a single history; it is a term in many histories. Anyone who writes the history of modern Germany, or of Poland, or of Nigeria, must deal with nationalism, but he will be concerned not with what is general in nationalism, but with what is peculiar to the nationalist experience of the history he is writing. And these peculiarities do not add up to 'nationalism as such'.

The first whale we must swallow is the assumption that nationalism is one single thing capable of explanation. In any concrete situation—

the career of Mr Lumumba in the Congo, or that of Kemal Atatürk in Turkey—the 'phenomena of nationalism' are so closely entwined with local circumstances as to be inexplicable without falling back on historical understanding. Nationalism is an abstraction; it is, more than that, an untidy and unrefined abstraction, and we must consequently expect that all attempts to produce a theory of it will generate abstract models put together on the principle that 'it takes an 'ism to explain an 'ism'.

These explanations consist of the production of factors or causes which have generated nationalist politics, and they come from every area of the social and human sciences. As we would expect, the topical importance of nationalism has induced every kind of specialist to step forward and contribute what light he can to the subject. In 1922, for example, when Irish nationalist struggles were just culminating in the establishment of Eire, the psycho-analyst Ernest Jones read a paper to the British Psycho-Analytical Society in which he presented an account of certain unconscious factors which he took to be important in Irish nationalism. His argument started from the observation that Ireland was an island, and that, like most islanders, the Irish conceived of their country as a Motherland. 'The complexes to which the idea of an island home tends to become attached are those relating to the ideas of woman, virgin, mother, and womb, all of which fuse in the central complex of the womb of the virgin mother.'[13] The English conquest of Ireland consequently appeared to the Irish in the guise of a mother raped, and consequently aroused a resentment beyond what could be satisfactorily explained simply in terms of a political grievance. Jones was not, of course, trying to *reduce* the history of Irish nationalism to a matter of unconscious passions; he was perfectly aware of the rational political superstructure of his subject matter. 'But I may perhaps be permitted to suggest', he concluded, 'that possibly history would have been different if England had had more inkling of the considerations here mentioned and had, instead of ravishing virgin Ireland as though she were a harlot, wooed her with the offer of an honourable alliance.'[14]

This kind of contribution to the psychology of nationalism is less common than one which begins from the assertion of a fundamental and innate tendency in all men to unite in groups. Hans Kohn, for example, suggests: 'The mental life of man is as much dominated by an ego-consciousness as it is by a group consciousness. Both are complex states of mind at which we arrive through experiences of differentiation and opposition, of the ego and the surrounding world, of the we-group and those outside the group.'[15] This theme may be developed into an exposition of group behaviour. Each group identifies itself by distinct ways of behaviour, and is likely to indulge its group cohesion by hostility to foreigners. One common accompaniment of nationalism is xenophobia. Many writers have assumed the existence of a tendency, almost a law of human behaviour, such that the greater the hostility to foreigners, the greater the cohesion of the group itself. In wartime, a country unites to defend itself, and falls to squabbling once the war is over. On this principle, the rulers of countries who find themselves faced with civil strife have been known to provoke external quarrels to avoid internal opposition. We would therefore expect that the development of a nation would be accompanied by aggressive and quarrelsome behaviour; and we might optimistically go further (like many nineteenth-century nationalists themselves) and hope that once the nation had firmly established itself, it would become far more peaceable in its behaviour without losing cohesion. This kind of theory sees nationalism as a kind of political adolescence.

It is true that some interesting comments can be made about nationalism along these lines. But this is a theory of group behaviour, of which nationalism is but one example. Psychological theories of this kind do not amount to explanations of nationalism as a distinct modern phenomenon.

It may seem odd to put the theologian alongside the psychologist as a theorist of nationalism; yet one of the commonest ways of trying to make sense of nationalism is to assimilate it to religion. On the face of it, this is a very sound approach to the matter, for the principles and concepts of European politics were heavily marked by theological ideas during the Middle Ages, and in modern times most prominent political ideas are close cousins of theology. The explanation of nationalism as a religion, however, starts not from intellectual analysis but from the observation of an inverse correlation: the fact that nationalism grew up in the world at just the moment when a religious view of reality was losing its grip on the minds of European men. As religion declined, so political ideologies, especially nationalism, advanced. Now if we add to this observation a psychological theory, in one form or another, that men have an innate need to serve something greater than themselves, then we are likely to conclude that, having abandoned the service of God, they had merely adopted the service of the nation. This kind of theory was most profoundly stated by Edmund Burke, who argued that European society with its kings, aristocrats and bishops, was not a random order of oppressors to be thrown off, but a structure created to satisfy human needs. Given this premise, kings, bishops and aristocrats, if overthrown, would have to be replaced by a set of substitutes—dictators or generals, commissars or professors. The interpretation of nationalism as a religion may be further reinforced by looking to the language of nationalists; it is often marked by a positively religious fervour. The analogies are nearly endless.

Yet they remain merely analogies. The basis of this view is the assumption of an unchanging human nature; and while human institutions do indeed exhibit a marked stability, it is not possible to describe this continuity except in terms so abstract that, in covering all cases of recorded human behaviour, they soon cease to tell us very much about any behaviour at all. The assertion that man must always seek to transcend himself, and having abandoned God he has now taken up the nation, is merely a different way of stating the very problem itself: namely that once men worshipped God and now they seem to worship the nation. But to the further question—Why the nation?—this view can give no answer. It thereby leaves us exactly where we started. In the process, it has elaborated the inverse correlation it began with into something far more than the evidence can bear. For it is perfectly clear, not only that many men have not abandoned religion, but also that many manage to combine nationalism *and* the worship of God; and the theory would only be really significant if the world were composed of nationalists *or* theists.

It would be foolish to conclude that psychology can throw no light upon nationalist phenomena. There are many teasing facts about nationalism which tempt us into trying out one category or another from psychology and seeing how it fits the facts. In virtually all cases of nationalism, we find a relation of weaker to stronger. Nationalities struggle to be free against powerful empires. This feeling of weakness is often ill-founded—the Germans experienced it towards the end of the nineteenth century when they were by any reckoning the most powerful state in Europe; and as Tilak was constantly pointing out to his supporters, the English in India were a tiny number in the midst of a sea of Indians. Nevertheless the feeling of weakness is often cultivated, in combination with the sense of grievance we discussed in the first chapter. Now a sense of grievance is useful to people in explaining why they have failed. Again, the sense of failure may be ill-founded. Yet in modern times all but the richest nations collectively experience a sense of their own inadequacy in a world for which they cannot feel themselves responsible. Nationalist theories may thus be understood as distortions of reality which allow men to cope with situations which they might otherwise find unbearable. As an account of this experience, consider this view of the psychology of the primitive African: 'The first time he ever came into contact with the white man, the African was simply overwhelmed, overawed, puzzled, perplexed, mystified, and dazzled. The white man's "houses that move on the water", his "bird that is not like other birds", his "monster that spits fire and smoke and swallows people and spits them out alive", his ability to "kill" a man and again raise him from the dead (anaesthesia), his big, massive and impressive house that had many other houses in it . . . and many new things introduced by the white man just amazed the African. . . . Here then the African came into contact with two-legged gods. . . .'[16] Now relationship with gods is easy: it consists in worshipping and obeying. However, as Nbabaningi Sithole goes on to describe, the white man comes to be regarded by the next generation of Africans not as a god but as a man. But he retains, by virtue of his skill and technology, many of the advantages he had before. Relationships with (contingently) superior men are a much more difficult matter. African nationalism, which commonly attributes such African 'inferiorities' as tribalism to the influence of the white man, would seem to be a way of coping with an unpleasant situation by the cultivation of grievances. In this way, the inferior may salvage a moral superiority. These are, as it were, two stages in relations between the West and the rest of the world; and one may hope to add a third stage in which, once a genuine equality has been attained, the practice of cultivating grievances may no longer be found necessary.

The most elaborate attempts to explain nationalism arise in the field of sociology, or such similar fields as social anthropology. We have already skirted round one such model of explanation in Chapter 4, pp. 83–85.[17] As an example of sociological explanation of nationalism, we might take Ernest Gellner's highly intricate argument in *Thought and Change*.[18] Gellner is typical in that he sees nationalism as a crucial element in a process of change leading from Traditional Society to Modern Society. Both the starting and finishing points of this process are highly abstract. Traditional Society is a category including everything from the European Middle Ages to the tribesmen of Africa, from the peasants of China to the nomads of the Mongolian steppes. Modern society is similarly elastic; its main characteristic is a developed industry, and consequently it cuts across other ideological boundaries to include life as it is lived in Washington or Moscow.

In order to simplify Gellner's highly complex argument, we may focus upon the image of the immigrant, a man who has left a traditional society and moved into a quite different world. The very type of modern immigrants has been the millions who moved from European villages to the United States of America, searching (as we are often told) for a better life. They leave behind a traditional society in which social economic and political relationships are generally determined by social *structure*. The transmission of property from one generation to another takes place not by expressing one's desires in a document called a will, but in accordance with longstanding custom. The kind of work a man can do depends upon the family he belongs to; and the selection of his wife is made within very narrow limits by parental decision and village tradition. What has impressed many observers about this kind of society is the fact that *choice* is very seldom exercised. Other observers have been impressed by the fact that villagers, by contrast with our modern day-dreaming populations who are always imagining themselves someone else, find it difficult to conceive of any other way of life. The point stressed by Gellner is that rigidity of structure makes communication between men comparatively unimportant; the peasant and the lord each know their business, and the fact that they may speak a different language results in no serious social, political or economic difficulties.

The immigrant moving into his America faces a quite new situation. No fixed structure exists by which he can live in a traditional pigeonhole or interpret the behaviour of other men. He can move around freely, and change jobs according to his hopes of enrichment. In this new situation, where social structure has largely gone, *culture* becomes far more important. Culture includes a manner of communication, in which language is central. Whereas in a stratified society, a plurality of languages presents little difficulty, in a modern society it would be crippling to social and economic life.

This account of the matter explains what—as Gellner emphasises —would otherwise be puzzling: nationalist concern with culture. 'Life is a difficult and serious business. The protection from starvation and insecurity is not easily achieved. In the achievement of it, effective government is an important factor. Could one think of a sillier, more *frivolous* consideration than the question concerning the native vernacular of the governors? Hardly: and men have seldom had time or taste for such curious frivolity.'[19] Yet obviously our immigrant-figure, whose life has become a matter of pursuing his opportunities, will find these opportunities much diminished if he cannot communicate with those around him, especially with those who govern him.

We have taken those who went to America as paradigms of the immigrant. But for our purposes, no such long journey was necessary. In the past the same experience was available to villagers who simply went off to the nearest town. Many of them did so on their own initiative; perhaps more felt driven by lack of land or a succession of famines. Acton's remark that 'exile is the nursery of nationality' cut deeper than he knew. The events of the last century, especially wars which led to the enrolment of native troops, had much the same disruptive effect upon traditional modes of life. But we may go further than this, and make the category of the immigrant even more abstract: we may observe that men may be drawn into the habits of the modern world even when they stay in the same place; they are 'spiritual immigrants' or, as Daniel Lerner remarks in expounding a different version of the same argument, they become 'psychically mobile'.[20]

These are the social changes which lead to nationalism. Gellner's argument develops at this point into a discussion of society as a machine for creating human beings. Isolated men who manage to survive in the jungle, it is well known, are barely distinguishable from animals; moral development, as Aristotle argued, requires a village, and indeed something larger than a village, if human potential is not to be stultified. Gellner's version of this argument is to observe that in modern conditions a fully developed human being has to be at least literate, and preferably also technically competent in the elementary respects familiar to anyone living in a large city. A village is economically incapable of supporting a system of education suitable to this task. Consequently social and political organisation must be conceived in much larger terms, such that modern and human cultural development may be achieved. For whilst in many previous civilisations literacy was the province of a specialist class, whose knowledge of Latin might allow them to move freely throughout Christendom, or Arabic might allow them to ignore political boundaries within Islam, in modern conditions *all* men must acquire this clerkly skill.

So far, the argument would explain why political loyalties in the modern world have changed their character, and expanded from a focus on the village or region to a focus on something a good deal larger. On this view, one might expect large empires to lose their local peculiarities and to become one single opportunity-area within which men moved freely. In fact, of course, the large empires have been broken up by nationalist education into smaller regions. Gellner explains this in terms of the uneven diffusion of the modernising process of industrialisation. Industrialisation is a painful process which began in Europe and America, with the agonies of child labour and long hours of work in dreary conditions; spread to Russia where the dictatorship of Stalin kept down the living standards of an entire generation in order to build up a potential of heavy industry; and has since been spreading over the rest of the globe. This unevenness of diffusion is found not only in the world at large, not only in great empires like the French and the British, but even within single countries themselves. In Britain the Highlands have been steadily depopulated; and in America for many decades the Deep South was industrially stagnant.

On Gellner's view, the political consequences of uneven industrialisation depend upon political conditions. Within a single country with a homogeneous population, men may move from the stagnant or underdeveloped areas and make their fortunes where industrialisation is under way. No cultural barrier is likely to stop them. But there are other, commoner circumstances in which the underdeveloped area is also characterised by having people of a different colour, or religion, or customs, or perhaps is at a distance from the industrialised area to which it is linked politically. Such is clearly the case with Asian and African colonies of European powers; but the same situation may happen within Europe itself. Under these circumstances, it will often be worthwhile for the small number of educated people in the underdeveloped area to split off their part of the world and to take over the leadership of this new area. 'Nationalism is not the awakening of nations to self-consciousness: it invents nations where they do not exist. . . .'[21] Gellner admits that a nationalist movement needs some pre-existing marks of a culture to work on; but the crucial characteristic of the new nation, on his argument, is the fact of its non-participation in the richer economic and political community.

Gellner's argument ignores the actual 'feel' of nationalism in favour of adumbrating a complex of social circumstances in which it will be intelligible. 'Men do not in general become nationalists from sentiment or sentimentality, atavistic or not, well-based or myth-founded: they become nationalists through genuine, objective, practical necessity, however obscurely recognised.'[22] Without taking the actual terms too literally, we may agree that social scientists seek to discern some kind of 'objective necessity' to explain nationalism. Our story of nationalist ideas has certainly been a story of the 'obscure recognition' of circumstances which made social and political life, unmodified, intolerable to those who lived it. Nationalism has been the first love of millions of men emerging into active political life for the first time; and they have been loath to be unfaithful.

7

Conclusion

Our discussion has been highly selective. A similar book might have been written with a quite different set of examples—Italy, pan-Slavism and modern France in Europe; Turkey, Japan, Egypt and Indonesia in the Afro-Asian world. But whatever the examples, we should have run into very similar difficulties with our material. The central difficulty stems from the common belief that nationalism is any form of political group-consciousness which takes an aggressive form. The world is full of groups—racial, tribal, religious, and traditional—and in the twentieth century, *all* of them will find the rhetoric of nationalism useful. But what is useful to politicians is often merely confusing to students of politics, and in this book we have been severe in our judgments of what constitutes nationalism.

Nationalism is a set of ideas, but as they travel from continent to continent, these ideas add up less to a theory than to a rhetoric, a form of self-expression by which a certain kind of political excitement can be communicated from an élite to the masses. These ideas are chameleons that take on the colour of the locality around them; we saw that German and Indian nationalists might use the same words and mean quite different things, and that nationalism combined with socialist ideas in Africa is radically different from nationalism combined with religion or state-worship in modern Europe.

If we try to find the core of nationalism, we encounter nothing more central than a paradox. The nature of this paradox may be elucidated by comparison with a much-discussed feature of the history of communism. Marxism predicted its own inevitable triumph in Western Europe where capitalism had ripened to full maturity; it in fact triumphed in Russia and China where capitalism was either just beginning or quite unknown.[1] The fact that Marxism, which purports to be a scientific theory elaborating a future of inevitable, economically determined events, should triumph only in those countries which *least* conform to the specifications of the theory —Russia and China—tells us a good deal about Marxist ideology which the ideology itself wishes to conceal: it tells us, in particular, that what is important is not the scientific character of the ideology but its power of inspiring political action. Now something similar is true of nationalism, which began by describing itself as the political and historical consciousness of the nation, and came in time to the inventing of nations for which it could act. The point we have had to emphasise about modern nationalism is that the politics comes first, and the national culture is constructed later. We have found nationalism without nations, aspirations substituted for reality. Instead of a dog beginning to wag its political tail, we find political tails trying to wag dogs. The Irish government tries to promote an Irish culture; the Nigerian government tries to persuade Ibos, Hausa, Fulanis and Yorubas that they are part of a Nigerian or an African nation; the Indian government attempts to mould Hindu and Muslim into citizens of a single nation.

This amounts to saying that the concept of the nation is almost entirely empty of content until a content is—arbitrarily—supplied from local circumstances. This is the reason why there is so much difficulty in trying to define a nation. This can only be done within a particular context. Our understanding of this point is obscured by nationalist ideology itself. Nationalists present their political struggle as one carried on by one homogeneous society against outside oppressors; but they then have to admit that these outside oppressors have internal allies—stooges, traitors, tribal and traditional habits of thought—in short, all that resists the national leadership itself. This nationalist self-characterisation is simply a misleading description of the fact that the nationalist process is a condition of civil war—and often, as we have seen, a civil war in which little notice is actually taken of the outside oppressor. Nationalistic rhetoric, often used by all parties to this civil struggle, is a strong card to play.

There is room for both the Sleeping Beauty and the Frankenstein's monster view of nationalism. It brings millions of people out of traditional corners into the global commerce of the modern world, and it induces a psychological climate conducive to bitter, irrational struggles over contested bits of territory. The good it does could all be done in other ways; but equally, it has contributed little more than a new vocabulary to the history of political evil.

References

CHAPTER I

1 Racialist thinkers have, however, hovered like vultures around the laboratory of anthropological inquiry, snatching here the corpse of a dead theory, there a raw lump of the living flesh. The absurdities of this farce in the history of European ideas are recounted in Jacques Barzun, *Race: A Study in Superstition*, rev. ed. New York 1965, esp. Ch. III.

2 E. H. Carr, *Nationalism and After*, Oxford 1945, p. 7.

3 I have discussed the similar role of the idea of 'society' in Ch. IV of *The Liberal Mind*, London 1963.

4 Elie Kedourie, *Nationalism*, London 1960, p. 72.

5 M. Philips Price, *A History of Turkey*, London 1956.

6 Hugh Trevor-Roper, *Jewish and other Nationalism*, London 1962, p. 19.

7 M. Philips Price, *op. cit.*, p. 113.

8 Richard Koebner and H. D. Schmidt, *Imperialism*, Cambridge 1964, p. 187.

9 C. M. Woodhouse, *The New Concert of Nations*, London 1964, p. 37.

10 Sharabi, *Nationalism and Revolution in the Arab World*, New Jersey 1966, pp. 156–7.

11 *Foreign Affairs*, vol. XVII, New York 1939, p. 316.

12 Hans Kohn, *Prophets and Peoples*, New York 1961, pp. 12–13.

13 Louis L. Snyder, *The Dynamics of Nationalism*, Princeton 1964, p. 29.

14 Kedourie, *op. cit.*, p. 9.

15 Ernst Nolte, *Three Faces of Fascism*, London 1965, p. 147.

16 Steven Runciman, *The Mediaeval Manichee*, Cambridge 1946, p. 98.

17 T. F. Tout, *The Empire and the Papacy*, London 1924, p. 73.

18 Beatrice Fry Hylop, *French Nationalism in 1789*, New York 1934, pp. 22–3.

19 J. L. Talmon, *The Unique and the Universal*, London 1965, p. 16.

20 *ibid.*, p. 13.

21 Hans J. Morgenthau, *Politics Among Nations*, New York 1961.

22 *The Economic Consequences of the Peace*, London 1919, pp. 29–30.

23 Kedourie, *op. cit.*, p. 87.

24 *The Big Fellow*, Dublin 1965, quote on p. 6 from Frank O'Connor, *Michael Collins and the Irish Revolution*.

25 Nolte, *op. cit.*, p. 79.

26 Elie Kedourie, 'Nationalism in the Middle East', in *Since 1945*, London 1966.

27 Greek National Assembly: Proclamation of Independence, 27 January 1822. Quoted in Hans Kohn (ed.), *Nationalism*, New York 1955.

28 Patrice Lumumba on the Independence of the Congo, 1960. Quoted in Hans Kohn and Wallace Sokolsky, *African Nationalism in the Twentieth Century*, New York 1966.

CHAPTER 2

1 The aspects of the eighteenth century which concern us here are brilliantly presented in Carl Becker, *The Heavenly City of the Eighteenth Century Philosophers*, Yale 1959.

2 *Encyclopédie*, entry *François ou Français*.

3 Alexis de Tocqueville, *L'Ancien Régime*, 1856, Bk. III, Ch. I.

4 *The Political Writings of Jean Jacques Rousseau*, ed. C. E. Vaughan, 2 vols., Cambridge 1915, vol. 1, p. 204.

5 *ibid.*, vol. 2, p. 427.

6 *ibid.*, vol. 2, p. 437.

7 See Jacques Barzun, *The French Race*, New York 1932, pp. 139–40.

8 Quoted by Barzun, *op. cit.*, p. 219.

9 *Qu'est-ce que le tiers état? par Emmanuel Sieyès, précédé de l'essai sur les privilèges*, Paris 1888. In citing *What is the Third Estate?*, I have used the translation by Jean Blondel, ed. S. E. Finer, introduction by Jack Lively, London 1963.

10 *What is the Third Estate?* p. 164.

11 *L'essai sur les privilèges*, p. 11 n.

12 *Third Estate*, p. 58.

13 *ibid.*, p. 126.

14 Carleton Hayes, *The Historical Evolution of Modern Nationalism*, New York 1948.

15 Stendhal, *Vie de Napoléon*, Paris 1962, p. 305. Italics in text.

16 Jules Michelet, *Historical View of the French Revolution*, quoted in Hans Kohn (ed.), *Nationalism*, New York 1955.

17 Carleton Hayes, *op. cit.*, p. 53.

18 *Third Estate*, p. 117.

19 *ibid.*, p. 74.

CHAPTER 3

1 *The Origins of Totalitarian Democracy*, 2nd ed., New York 1958, p. 183.

2 E. J. Hobsbawm, *The Age of Revolution, 1789–1848*, New York 1963, p. 167.

3 Joseph Mazzini, *The Duties of Man*.

4 Hans Kohn, *The Mind of Germany*, London 1965, p. 198.

5 *ibid.*, p. 90.

6 Mazzini, *op. cit.* See also Gaetano Salvemini, *Mazzini*, London 1956 (1st Italian ed. 1905), p. 42.

7 J. L. Talmon, *The Unique and the Universal*, London 1965, p. 97.

8 See F. Barnard, *Herder's Social and Political Thought*, Oxford 1965.

9 Talmon, *op. cit.*, p. 100.

10 Quoted Barnard, *op. cit.*, p. 58.

11 Quoted Kohn, *op. cit.*, p. 77.

12 *ibid.*

13 Quoted Barnard, *op. cit.*, p. 59.

14 Kedourie, *Nationalism*, p. 31.

15 A. J. P. Taylor, *The Course of German History*, London 1961, p. 39.

16 H. S. Reiss, *The Political Thought of the German Romantics, 1793–1815*, Oxford 1955, p. 94.

17 *ibid.*, p. 17.

18 *ibid.*, p. 99.

19 *ibid.*, pp. 115–16.

20 *ibid.*, p. 105.

21 *ibid.*, p. 105.

22 Heinrich von Treitschke, *In Memory of the Great War*, 1895. Quoted in Louis Snyder, *The Dynamics of Nationalism*, Princeton 1964, pp. 163–4.

23 Kohn, *op. cit.*, p. 78.

24 Snyder, *op. cit.*, pp. 146–7.

25 *ibid.*, p. 146.

26 *ibid.*, p. 136.

27 Kohn, *op. cit.*, Ch. 8.

28 *ibid.*, p. 184.

29 See Fritz Stern, *The Politics of Cultural Despair*, Berkeley 1961.

30 G. L. Mosse, *The Crisis of German Ideology*, London 1966, pp. 4–5.

31 *ibid.*, especially Ch. 2.

32 Stern, *op. cit.*, pp. 91–2.

33 Kohn, *op. cit.*, p. 204.

34 *ibid.*, p. 205.

35 Stern, *op. cit.*, p. 101.

36 *ibid.*, p. 91.

37 Quoted Talmon, *op. cit.*, p. 159.

CHAPTER 4

1 W. Wedderburn, *Allan Octavian Hume: Father of The Indian National Congress*, London 1913.

2 See Daniel Lerner, *The Passing of Traditional Society*, Glencoe, Illinois 1958.

3 See Michael Banton, *Roles: An Introduction to the Study of Social Relations*, London 1965.

4 See Joseph R. Levenson, *Confucian China and its Modern Fate*, London 1964, 3 vols. I have used a few elements of vol. 1 of this brilliant work.

5 R. P. Masani, *Dadabhai Naoraji*, London 1938, pp. 229–30.

6 Dadabhai Naoraji, *Speeches and Writings*, Madras, n.d.

7 From *Speeches and Writings of Hon. Surendranath Banerjee*, p. 228. Quoted in Wm. Theodore de Bary, *et al.*, *Sources of Indian Tradition*, New York 1958.

8 *Speeches of the Honourable Mr G. K. Gokhale*, pp. 741–5. Quoted in de Bary, *op. cit.*, pp. 699–700.

9 Quoted from the journal *Comrade* by de Bary, *op. cit.*, p. 774.

10 See Karan Singh, *Prophet of Indian Nationalism*, London 1963.

11 Gandhi, *Communal Unity*, p. 217. Quoted de Bary, p. 824.

12 Gandhi, *Hind Swaraj*. Quoted de Bary, p. 804.

13 *ibid.*, p. 812.

14 C. F. Andrews, *Letters to a Friend*, p. 128. Quoted de Bary, p. 791.

15 *ibid.*, p. 792.

16 Rabindranath Tagore, 'The Call of Truth', *Modern Review*, xxx, 4, pp. 429–33. Quoted de Bary, p. 793.

17 Quoted Nehru, *Towards Freedom*, New York 1942, p. 314.

18 Tagore, *op. cit.* Quoted de Bary, pp. 793–5.

19 *ibid.*, p. 794.

20 Colin Legum, *Pan-Africanism. A Short Political Guide*, rev. ed. London 1965, p. 36.

21 See, for example, Cheikh Anta Diop, *The Cultural Contributions and Prospects of Africa*, 1956. A longish extract is printed in Hans Kohn and Wallace Sokolsky, *African Nationalism in the Twentieth Century*, New York 1965.

22 See Legum, *op. cit.*, p. 235.

23 See Kwame Nkrumah, *Autobiography*, Edinburgh 1957.

24 *The Party*, No. 19, 16–28 February 1962, p. 11. Quoted Kohn and Sokolsky, *op. cit.*, p. 185.

25 Appendix 22 of Legum, *op. cit.*, p. 278.

26 Nkrumah, *op. cit.*, p. ix.

27 Legum, *op. cit.*

28 Brian Crozier, *The Morning After*, London 1963.

29 Quoted Kohn and Sokolsky, *op. cit.*, p. 182.

CHAPTER 5

1 Hans Kohn, *The Mind of Germany*, London 1965, p. 91.

2 See Barzun article.

3 See Karl Deutsch, *Nationalism and Social Communication*, Cambridge, Mass., 2nd ed. 1966, p. 97.

4 Mary C. Bromage, *De Valera and the March of a Nation*, London 1956, p. 226.

5 Legum, *op. cit.*, p. 216.

6 See Brian Crozier, *The Morning After*, London 1963.

CHAPTER 6

1 Lord Acton, *Nationality*. See Gertrude Himmelfarb (ed.), *Essays on Freedom and Power*, New York 1965, p. 146.

2 J. S. Mill, *Considerations on Representative Government*, Ch. XVI.

3 Acton, *op. cit.* All quotations from Acton in this section are from the essay on *Nationality*.

4 Mill, *op. cit.*, p. 385.

5 See the discussion in Shirley Robin Letwin, *The Pursuit of Certainty*, Cambridge 1965, p. 367, from which this quotation is taken.

6 See David Shub, *Lenin*, London 1966, Ch. 7.

7 Isaac Deutscher, *Stalin*, London 1966, rev. ed., pp. 476–7.

8 Joseph Stalin, *Marxism and the National Question*, New York 1942, p. 38.

9 *ibid.*, p. 19.

10 *ibid.*, pp. 22–3.

11 Deutscher, *op. cit.*, p. 187.

12 *ibid.*, p. 190.

13 Ernest Jones, *Essays in Applied Psycho-Analysis*, London 1951, p. 98.

14 *ibid.*, p. 111.

15 Hans Kohn, *The Idea of Nationalism*, New York 1944, p. 11.

16 Ndabaningi Sithole, *African Nationalism*, New York 1959, p. 146. Quoted Snyder, *op. cit.*, p. 344.

17 See, for example, Daniel Lerner, *The Passing of Traditional Society*, Glencoe, Illinois 1958.

18 Ernest Gellner, *Thought and Change*, London 1964, esp. Ch. 7.

19 *ibid.*, p. 153.

20 Lerner, *op. cit.*, Ch. II.

21 Gellner, *op. cit.*, p. 168.

22 *ibid.*, p. 160.

CHAPTER 7

1 K. R. Popper, *The Open Society and its Enemies*, vol. 2, Ch. 15, § III.

A Note on
Further Reading

Among many general studies of nationalism, Elie Kedourie's *Nationalism* may be mentioned as outstanding. Frederick Hertz, *Nationality in History and Politics: A Study of the Psychology and Sociology of National Sentiment and Character* is less sophisticated, but is a mine of suggestive information. Boyd Shafer, *Nationalism: Myth and Reality*; Hans Kohn, *The Idea of Nationalism*; Louis L. Snyder, *The Meaning of Nationalism*; and Carleton J. H. Hayes, *The Historical Evolution of Modern Nationalism* are among many useful studies of a general kind. Nationalism may also usefully be studied by the use of 'readings', such as: Louis L. Snyder, *The Dynamics of Nationalism*; Colin Legum, *Pan-Africanism*; Sylvia Haim, *Arab Nationalism*; Hans Kohn, *Nationalism*; and Elie Kedourie, *Nationalism in Asia and Africa*.

No understanding of nationalism is possible without a good deal of historical information, at least of the kind found in such general surveys as: David Thomson, *Europe since Napoleon*; H. Hearder, *Europe in the Nineteenth Century*; E. J. Hobsbawm, *The Age of Revolution, 1789–1848*; and W. C. Easton, *The Rise and Fall of Western Colonialism*.

Nationalism is best understood in its local context, and this may be the intellectual traditions of a country, considered in such books as: Hans Kohn, *The Mind of Germany* or Herbert Tint, *The Decline of French Patriotism*; in addition, modern political scientists have studied nationalist politics in virtually every country and region of the world—producing a useful series of books, marred in some cases by a disposition to see nationalism everywhere. Finally, we may mention, as examples of an attempt to give a scientific explanation of nationalism, Karl Deutsch, *Nationalism and Social Communication*; Daniel Lerner, *The Passing of Traditional Society*; Florian Znaniecki, *Modern Nationalities*; and, more philosophically, Ernest Gellner, *Thought and Change*.

Index

of Names and Nations

(Dates of birth and death have been supplied in appropriate cases.)